PERFORMANCE INDICATORS FOR LOCAL ANTI-DRUGS STRATEGIES – A PRELIMINARY ANALYSIS

Mike Chatterton
Gwendy Gibson
Mark Gilman
Christine Godfrey
Matthew Sutton
Alan Wright

POLICE RESEARCH GROUP
CRIME DETECTION AND PREVENTION SERIES: PAPER NO 62
LONDON: HOME OFFICE POLICE DEPARTMENT

Editor: Barry Webb
Home Office Police Research Group
50 Queen Anne's Gate
London SW1H 9AT

Police Research Group: Crime Detection and Prevention Series

The Home Office Police Research Group (PRG) was formed in 1992 to carry out and manage research relevant to the work of the police service. The terms of reference for the Group include the requirement to identify and disseminate good policing practice.

The Crime Detection and Prevention Series follows on from the Crime Prevention Unit papers, a series which has been published by the Home Office since 1983. The recognition that effective crime strategies will often involve both crime prevention and crime investigation, however, has led to the scope of this series being broadened. This new series will present research material on both crime prevention and crime detection in a way which informs policy and practice throughout the service.

A parallel series of papers on resource management and organisational issues is also published by PRG, as is a periodical on policing research called 'Focus'.

ISBN 1-85893-391-9

Foreword

The illicit use of drugs presents police forces with one of the most pressing current crime problems. The high priority given to tackling the problem is reflected by the substantial amount of resources committed to it by the police and other agencies, the national Key Objectives for the police and the Government's recently published White Paper Tackling Drugs Together.

In order to develop effective drug strategies, it is important that forces use performance indicators which monitor the impact of the strategy and ways in which it might be improved. The Police Research Group therefore commissioned research to identify indicators that would provide such information to local managers.

The research is being conducted in two phases. The first phase is to identify the broad areas where indicators should be sought, and the feasability of developing indicators in these areas. The second phase is to actively develop and test the suitability of a suite of indicators within a force which is implementing a drug strategy.

This paper reports the findings from the first phase of the research. It examines how the performance of different aspects of forces strategies, such as diversion and enforcement activity, might be measured and the extent to which performance indicators might be constructed from operational data already being collected by the police. An important characteristic of performance indicators is that the data required to provide them should be capable of being collected by forces relatively easily. The report of the second phase of the work, which will present a list of proposed performance indicators, should be available by the end of the year.

I M BURNS
Deputy Under Secretary of State
Home Office
Police Department
May 1995

Acknowledgements

Grateful thanks are expressed to a number of people who provided help and information for this research.

To Mr Wilmot, Chief Constable of the Greater Manchester Police without whose co-operation this study would not have been possible and who recognised the requirement for more research in the drugs field some considerable time ago. To Mr Cairns, Deputy Chief Constable of the Greater Manchester Police and to former Assistant Chief Constables Hamilton and Jolly for their assistance in setting up the project and facilitating liaison with units within the force. To the heads of the three territorial divisions, community relations and CID. We particularly wish to single out Chief Inspector Ron Clarke who always found time within a crippling itinerary to confer with us.

We should like to express a special debt of gratitude to all those officers and support staff in the GMP and the Dedicated Drugs Unit who were so generous with their advice and information.

Our thanks are also due to Sergeant Mark Granby of the Greater Manchester Police who produced the section of the report on custody officers, to Professor Ken Pease for his advice on the statistical analysis, to the staff of the Faculty of Economic and Social Studies' Data Preparation Unit, to Tony Green for his conscientious data collection, to Samantha Frenz for her involvement in the early stages of the project and to Rebecca Kelly and Alex Turner for their assistance in creating order out of chaos and transforming our efforts into a report.

Particular thanks to Warwick Maynard for helpful advice and support throughout the project and particularly regarding the format of the report.

Henry Fielding Centre, Manchester University
Centre for Health Economics, York University

The Authors

Mike Chatterton, Gwendy Gibson and Alan Wright are members of the Henry Fielding Centre at the University of Manchester.

Christine Godfrey and Matthew Sutton are members of the Centre for Health Economics at the University of York.

Mark Gilman is responsible for prevention and development at Manchester's LIFELINE.

Executive summary

Issues

The introduction of a Drugs Strategy in the Greater Manchester Police (GMP) in October 1993 provided an opportunity to investigate the effects of its constituent enforcement and harm reduction measures. It was intended that the performance indicators developed for the purposes of this evaluation would be capable of being applied by police forces across the country in developing their drug strategies.

The first three sections of the report describe the complex and variable form that enforcement measures, harm reduction initiatives and drugs markets can take. A strategic approach to drugs problems needs to understand how these three areas, and the organisations within them, impact upon each other. Which type of drug abuser or dealer for example, is affected by which type of law enforcement intervention and how are they affected? It is conceivable that the level of impact of any such initiative varies, in as yet unknown ways, according to the characteristics of dealing organisations and of the drugs users identified in this part of the report. Deployment decisions would be easier if policy makers knew for certain which measures have the greatest harm reduction impact.

Evidence discussed on the relationship between drugs and crime is shown to be inconclusive. Claims that there is a strong connection are contested in other parts of the literature, on the grounds that they fail to establish an unequivocal, one-way causal link. They are also criticised for exaggeration.

Different types of performance indicator are identified in these earlier sections of the report. Some indicators attempt to provide information on the more intangible, eventual outcomes of interventions. Others, operating at the opposite end of the spectrum, relate to inputs and the quality of system processes which determine how those resources are used. Output indicators probe the more immediate results of activity.

The design of an indicator must be informed by a decision about its intended use. Evaluators may wish to compare a particular unit's levels of performance at different time periods or they may want to compare it with similar units during the same time period. Alternatively, the performance of units may be less relevant than the effectiveness of intervention methods. A key issue, for example, may be whether certain tactics produce better outcomes than others.

Input and process indicators are invaluable sources of information about systems and resource inputs which directly affect outputs and outcomes. In fact, the report argues, they provide the context within which the information provided by output and outcome indicators has to be interpreted. We can only begin to understand **what** has been achieved by investigating **how** it was achieved which means placing it in this context.

The report also discusses the role of factors external to an organisation which can affect its performance but over which it may have little or no control.

The research

Several pieces of empirical research were conducted during the project to investigate the issues discussed earlier, to identify relevant, robust and feasible indicators and to audit the quality of the information systems within the force, that might service them. This research also aimed to provide base-line data on the immediate post-implementation period of the strategy enabling comparisons to be made of the effects of the strategy later on. The remaining sections of the report describe the findings of these pieces of research.

Two small surveys were conducted to examine the drug markets on the B, C, and M Divisions in GMP which were selected as target divisions for data collection purposes. 38 self-completion questionnaires were completed by drug-users and 12 heroin users were interviewed in-depth about the availability of drugs and changes that might be associated with the introduction of the strategy. The interviews revealed that a rapid delivery system was provided by dealers who were contactable by mobile telephone and whose business depended on the speed of their delivery and the quality of their product. The market was described as a buyers'-market which offered easy access to all types of drugs. There was no evidence from this small number of interviews, that the strategy had affected the drugs market.

The drugs-crime connection was examined through the use of a survey of arresting officers on the three target divisions. They were asked to report any evidence suggesting that the person they had arrested was involved in drug use or dealing. Apart from its intrinsic interest, it was considered that this material might provide an outcome indicator. Once the strategy begins to bite, through its enforcement and referral elements, it is to be anticipated that there will be a decrease in the proportion of those people arrested who are drug abusers or dealers.

A drugs connection was established in 19% of the arrest cases. The connection was higher for some offences than others and in cases where the arrested person's premises had been searched eg. in 42% of burglary arrests.

Base line data and a possible second outcome indicator, were developed through a matching exercise. "Attributor" information on anonymous individuals recorded on the Regional Drugs Misuse Data Base, was matched against "attributor" data relating to all persons arrested on one of the target divisions. If the effectiveness of the referral system in directing people to treatment increases, there should be a corresponding increase in the proportion of matches.

The strategy makes custody sergeants responsible for the issuing of referral cards and almost a half of the custody sergeants in the force were interviewed. They were asked about the strategy and the referral system and how the latter worked in practice. The findings demonstrate the importance of investigating systems which can have an intervening effect between the strategy and its outputs and outcomes. (A small number of interviews were held with health and social care personnel for similar reasons). Only 18% of sergeants issued cards to every arrested person as the strategy required.

Arrests for drug offences on the three target divisions during a pre-implementation and post-implementation period were analysed. The "demonstration analysis" revealed that it was impossible to assess certain effects of the strategy because of gaps in the recorded data. For example, the department or function of the arresting officer was not always recorded in police records. Both arrests and arrest events could be counted as outputs and the analysis revealed the implications of taking one or the other as an output measure.

Information on the circumstances leading up to arrests is needed to assess whether, and to what extent, arrests reflect changes in enforcement style consistent with the requirements of the strategy. The research has demonstrated that this information is expensive to collect and that it is not yet available in a standardised format.

Arrests by the drugs squad were analysed in greater detail – again comparing a pre-implementation and a post-implementation period. Seizure data ie the amount and type of drugs involved in each arrest, and the charges brought against those arrested, suggest that many of the arrests made by the squad were "incongruous" given the squad's strategic mandate to target on major traffickers in Class A drugs. However, it is just possible that many of those arrested were in fact major dealers, who for a variety of reasons, were in possession of small quantities of Class "B" drugs when they were arrested. Had the squad operated with a clearly defined target classification system it would have been possible to check this out, but the system was difficult to assess and confusing to use. Interviews with members of the squad revealed that they were uncertain about the categories and the targets they were working on.

These are important findings.

Unless targets and objectives are explicitly stated from the outset of an operation, not only is it impossible to decide whether effort has been appropriately targeted but, perhaps more important, without this information it is difficult to see how the data produced by output indicators can be interpreted. These problems of interpretation are magnified when output data are aggregated, for example on drug arrests made by a number of units that have different objectives and are focused on different levels of targets.

A key issue for further investigation is the extent to which the police can exercise control over intervening variables which otherwise determine how successful they are in the drugs field, and if they can, whether they are exercising that control in practice.

The intrusion of factors external to the organisation attenuates the link between objectives and outputs. During the course of the research examples were found of drugs enforcement operations failing because of the intervention of such factors. In other instances, however, the source of the failure lay inside the organisation, in the systems that the unit depended upon for its effectiveness. Several of these systems are identified in the report and the possibility of developing indicators relating to the performance of these systems is discussed.

The final section of the report provides an audit of the information currently available in force for performance monitoring.

Contents

List of Tables

List of Figures

1. Introduction

Background

In tackling drug misuse the police do not work in isolation. Drug policy involves a complex interaction between the police and the criminal justice system, health and social care services and the drugs market. The purpose of this report is to illustrate how these interactions affect attempts to measure police interventions and to suggest how objective indicators of the success of police interventions might be developed.

The history of drugs policy in recent years has often highlighted competing enforcement and harm-reduction approaches to the problems of illicit drug use and drug-related crime. The lack of objective data has made it impossible to assess the extent to which these police and other agency interventions have had a significant impact on drug-related harm. No conceptually rigorous and empirically grounded models exist of the interactions between drug markets, police activity, other agencies and the consequent social outcomes.

Project objectives

The overall aim of the project was to develop objective indicators which could be used to evaluate police interventions in the drug market, and to predict outcomes in terms of drug-related crime and other social costs. This work included developing a framework for describing the interactive links between the police, the rest of the criminal justice system, health and social care agencies, and drug markets.

The specific objectives of the project were:

* To identify performance measures which could be used to assess the effect of initiatives taken in the various areas covered by the Greater Manchester Police drugs strategy;

* To provide an audit of information sources relevant to performance measurement in the above areas and to make recommendations for change if requirements were not fully met by existing information systems;

* To establish base-line data relating to a period of time before the force drugs strategy was introduced and a second period covering the first months of its implementation. It was recognised that only a limited evaluation of the effects of the strategy would be possible during the project. Some comparative analysis was, however, to be undertaken to demonstrate the approach and the methods that could be employed to evaluate certain parts of the strategy in future;

* To investigate the requirements to be met if the aims of the strategy were to be achieved. This would entail an examination of 'input' prerequisites, broadly

defined to include the provision of training, appropriate management systems etc. Systematic measurement of inputs, through such methods as activity analysis was, however, beyond the scope of the project.

Greater Manchester Police drugs misuse strategy

The development of the GMP drugs misuse strategy provided a useful opportunity to begin empirical work on devising indicators of the success of police anti-drugs work. The strategy was introduced against a background of changing drug problems in Manchester. Heroin and crack distribution has become more centralised, particularly in the part of inner-city Manchester that is arguably the most difficult to police: Moss Side and Hulme. The marketplace has become more dangerous for both users and dealers, the latter having become engaged in territorial disputes resulting in violence and a number of murders in these areas. As the demand for crack has grown amongst heroin users, responsibility for the supply has been taken up by heroin retailers. By 1988, Moss Side was recognised as the centre for the purchase of heroin and by 1992 crack was also widely available in this area. Many users who purchase their drugs in Moss Side are now using heroin to alleviate the side effects of the use of crack. In order to avoid painting a distorted picture, it should be noted that the increase in the use of crack in these areas has not been experienced to the same extent elsewhere in Greater Manchester.

The centralisation of heroin and crack dealing in Moss Side and Hulme was a major problem for the police. Police-community relations were strained and information about heroin and crack dealing was not as forthcoming as it had been in the era of user-dealer networks. Nevertheless, police mounted several operations, 'Corkscrew' and 'China' against heroin, and 'Miracle' against crack, which were targeted upon local dealers working mainly on the streets.

Empirical work carried out for the Home Office (Chatterton et al, 1992) confirmed that drug activity extended to adjacent areas including Hulme and Whalley Range. The effect upon local residents, caused by a range of factors from discarded syringes to social disruption by street dealing, led to fear of crime, particularly fear of victimisation in crimes of violence.

Mobile telephones and pager systems have become the norm for ordering heroin and crack which is delivered by courier on mountain bike locally, or by car further afield. Recent developments have included the 'cloning' of a number of stolen mobile telephones by reprogramming the electronic chip, thus enabling any courier working for a major dealer to respond quickly to the customer. This emulation of a flexible business approach illustrates the extent to which the market is capable of adapting to new opportunities. The speed and secrecy of these new methods further frustrates police efforts.

In 1992, the GMP formed a working party to examine the relationship between crime and illegal drug use, particularly heroin. They noted that between 1981 and 1991, there had been increases in the volume of reported acquisitive crime, the number of registered heroin addicts and the perceived illegal street supply of heroin. Consultation with a number of drug agencies identified average daily addict consumption at a gramme per day, an average street price of £80 per gramme, and the existence of an equal number of non-registered to registered heroin addicts. The working party thus calculated that the turnover in illegal heroin in Greater Manchester is in excess of £42 million per year. Assuming a re-sale value for stolen goods of one third of retail price, the group concluded that the potential cost to the Greater Manchester community exceeded £126 million per annum.

The working group concluded that the so-called 'war on drugs', based for the past two decades on a prohibitionist policy, had failed to stem the increase in the supply of Class A substances on the street, particularly heroin and crack. It was argued that the concentration on what were primarily enforcement measures had marginalised drug users, resulting in the deterioration of their health while increasing the cost to society through acquisitive crime. The group acknowledged that while the police had a major role to play in enforcing drugs legislation, this approach had not adequately addressed the problem of demand reduction.

A force drugs misuse strategy based on the working group conclusion was developed with the intention to reduce the supply of drugs available and raise public confidence by implementing "strong policies" towards drug traffickers; to reduce the incidence of drug related crime; to address the demand for drugs and reduce the harm caused to both the user and the wider community; and to contribute to the prevention of the spread of HIV/AIDS and other associated illnesses.

Organising enforcement: the Broome model

The report of the Association of Chief Police Officers working party on drug-related crime (1986) – the Broome Report – claimed that drugs markets are pyramidic in character, with major dealers and importers operating at the pinnacle, middle level distributors in a middle-tier, and street-level dealers in the lowest tier. The research by Dorn et al, 1992; Wright and Waymont, 1989; Wright et al, 1993, demonstrated that the pyramidic model neither reflected the dynamics of the drugs markets nor the way that drugs squads actually work. Wright et al (1993), suggested that a flexible two-tier system would be a more appropriate design. Enlarged dedicated drugs units and police force drugs squads would concentrate at the supply end of the market. Street level enforcement would continue through the deployment of divisional drugs units. It was this amended two-tier version of Broome which was adopted as the basis of the GMP force anti-drugs strategy.

The GMP strategy tasked the force drugs squad with the responsibility for targeting major drugs suppliers and dealers across the force area. Divisional plain clothes units were given responsibility for working on 'dealers' operating within their divisional boundaries and this could include 'major dealers'.

Structure of the report

In the second section of this report, an attempt is made to clarify some of the issues surrounding the use of performance indicators in this context. Some terms often used in discussions about performance indicators are defined and described. It is vital that the purpose of performance measurement is clearly defined, and that appropriate performance indicators are adopted which reflect these concerns.

Section 3 contains a description of the drugs problem which police work aims to tackle: drug markets and the links with other crimes. A review of the literature suggests that the drugs market is complex and dynamic, as are the links with other types of crime. It is recommended that types of drug dealing and drug use be described along a number of dimensions. These dimensions may be measured using information gathered through intelligence and surveillance operations, or through independent soundings. The results of two pilot user surveys are presented. The ability of arresting police officers to identify which other crimes may be drug-related is investigated, and mechanisms by which this process can be improved are detailed.

Police anti-drugs strategies will have many components. In this study, diversion and enforcement strategies have been investigated, and these are dealt with in sections 4 and 5. In both sections, the ways in which activity is organised are outlined. Empirical work concentrated on investigating process through qualitative interviews, and some measurement of output using existing information databases is attempted. Concluding each of these sections are summaries of indicators which may be appropriate for different types of output.

The last section of this report covers the results of an initial information audit and a tentative set of process, output and outcome indicators for further testing.

2. Issues in performance measurement

Under the umbrella of performance measurement it is possible to ask a whole range of different questions, and it is crucial to develop the right indicator for each problem. Analyses could address comparisons between units, ie. whether:

(i)   a particular enforcement unit appears to be performing better than in the last period

(ii)   in a particular period, one enforcement unit appears to be performing better than a similar one in a different area

or comparisons between different types of intervention, ie. whether there is evidence to suggest that:

(iii) one enforcement approach performs better than an alternative one (such as the choice of targeting small or large-scale dealers)

(iv)   the enforcement approach performs better than alternative police approaches

(v)   the police approach to drug problems performs better than non-police approaches

Attributes of good performance indicators

The Government Green Paper, *Tackling Drugs Together* (1994), suggests six criteria for indicators of the performance of agencies involved in drugs policy: relevance (agencies can influence the indicators relating to their work); boundedness (a maximum of six indicators are used); comprehensiveness; validity; reliability (the accuracy of indicators is acceptable); and consistency (validity over time).

Performance indicators clearly need to be measurable, although measurement in some cases may need to be qualitative. If indicators are to be useful in changing the mix of anti-drug activities to achieve the most desirable social outcomes, then the responsibility for affecting different indicators and incentives for achieving good performance needs to be established. Other requirements should be that indicators and monitored activities are linked, and that changes can be evaluated.

Types of indicators: input, process, output and outcome

Input

Analysis of input is concerned with the level of resources. For enforcement activity, inputs include the amount of equipment available and total whole-time equivalent staff. The volume of input should be adjusted for quality factors, such as surveillance training received by officers and the standard of the equipment available. For referral schemes, inputs will include the number of treatment slots available and levels, grades and continuity of staffing in the health/social care sector.

Process

Given a level of input, management and organisational decisions will affect how those resources are used to create different types of process. Process measures will include concepts such as: the number of person-hours of surveillance undertaken, target identification processes, and briefing and de-briefing sessions.

Outputs

Outputs are the intermediate results of police activity. Successful anti-drug operations will result in arrests and seizures of drugs. The output of providing an arrested and cautioned drug user with information on drugs services could be measured by their entry into treatment. Other output measures may reflect the 'turning' of informants for future operations, or seizures of assets under the Drug Trafficking Offences Act, 1986.

Outcomes

The outcomes of drug enforcement and diversion interventions represent the ultimate end-products of these activities. Improvements in outcome may be measured by reductions in drug-related harm or in the social costs of illicit drug use. A range of possible dimensions of drug-related harm are listed in Table 1.

Table 1: Harms with which drug misuse is associated

DIMENSION	TYPE OF HARM
CRIME	Committed under the influence
	Committed to buy drugs
	Disputes over drug market transactions
	Contacts made in criminal society
HEALTH	Overdoses
	Accidents whilst under the influence
	HIV risk
	Hepatitis B and C
	Poisoning through adulterants
	Abscesses, ulcers and sores
	Thrombosis
	Effects of drugs themselves
	Poor drug-using lifestyles
	Addiction
	Effect on babies' health
EMPLOYMENT/ EDUCATION	Qualifications obtained
	Jobs selection
	Chances of securing work
	Productivity and sickness absence
SOCIAL	Pain and suffering of friends/family
	Effect on local environment

Relationships between input, process, output, outcome and external factors

For police anti-drug activity, four stages in the translation of resources into desirable outcomes have been identified. Indicators can be developed to measure performance at each of these stages. External factors will affect production at these stages, and some of these are shown in Figure 1 which summarises the process.

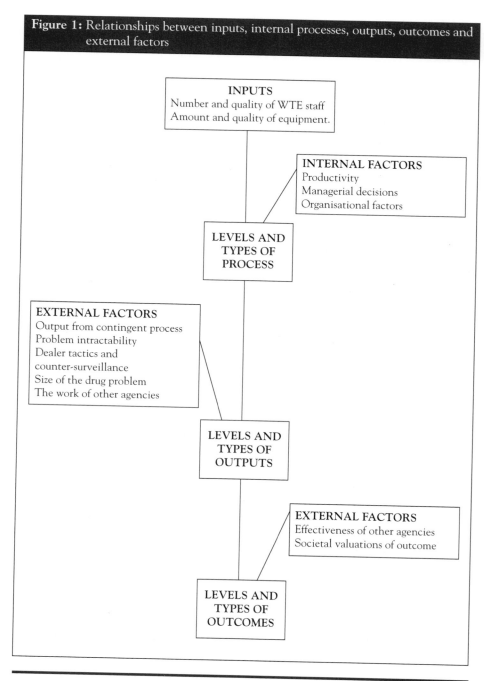

Figure 1: Relationships between inputs, internal processes, outputs, outcomes and external factors

INPUTS
Number and quality of WTE staff
Amount and quality of equipment.

INTERNAL FACTORS
Productivity
Managerial decisions
Organisational factors

LEVELS AND TYPES OF PROCESS

EXTERNAL FACTORS
Output from contingent process
Problem intractability
Dealer tactics and
counter-surveillance
Size of the drug problem
The work of other agencies

LEVELS AND TYPES OF OUTPUTS

EXTERNAL FACTORS
Effectiveness of other agencies
Societal valuations of outcome

LEVELS AND TYPES OF OUTCOMES

Units and periods of analysis

The units and periods of analysis should be chosen to reflect the purpose of the analysis, and to meet the required attributes of good performance indicators. The performance of enforcement activity can be assessed at the micro or macro-level. A list of potential units of analysis which might be evaluated or compared include: individuals, units, divisions, squads, forces, and activity at the national level.

Evaluations may concentrate on activity over different time-periods. An example, cited as demonstrating the problems involved in measuring the effectiveness of police operations against drugs, is that of a 'controlled buy' operation which fails to produce a 'result', as the target supplier does not show up at the arranged meeting time (Pearson, 1990). If a nil result occurred in a large proportion of cases, 'controlled buy' operations may not be a good use of scarce resources. More appropriately, individual operations should be assessed on the probability of a successful outcome, a concept which would be measurable over a larger number of operations.

If a number of such operations should fail, the key question is whether this should be taken as an indicator of the ineffectiveness of the 'controlled buy' tactic. Before abandoning what could, in fact, be a very powerful weapon in the law enforcement arsenal, it would be necessary to consider whether other factors were preventing it from being used effectively and whether these could be controlled.

Throughout the report, attention will be drawn to two distinct types of intervening factors which determine whether strategies and tactics achieve their desired goals; exogenous (or external) and endogenous factors. Exogenous factors lie outside the direct control of enforcement and treatment agencies. They include such variables as the sophistication of target criminals, their surveillance consciousness, their level of organisation, the extensiveness of their networks, etc. Similarly, influences in the personal lives of heroin addicts, such as peer-pressures and relationships may have a greater effect upon their willingness to enter a methadone programme than anything agencies say and do. Endogenous factors are much more under the control of the agencies in question. If it is to be successfully employed, a particular tactic needs to be adequately resourced, the quality of the inputs needs to be good and staff need to be competently organised, briefed and led. If these internal requirements are not satisfied, then the tactical intervention is more likely to fail. In learning organisations, where the culture encourages people to learn from mistakes and failures in a constructive and non-blaming way, the role of such endogenous factors in explaining failure is more likely to be identified. In agencies which have not developed such a culture, failure is more likely to be attributed to the tactic itself – the 'nothing works' malaise – or to exogenous factors (Chatterton, 1987; Pedlar, Burgoyne and Boydell, 1991).

Purposes of performance measurement and appropriate indicators

Performance measurement most often takes the form of unit comparisons (questions of types (i) or (ii) listed at the beginning of this chapter). Units are often compared on the level of output they produce (Tackling Drugs Together, 1994). However, as shown in Figure 1, it is invalid to base conclusions about productivity or efficiency on output measures, without acknowledging the effects of background and contextual factors. Furthermore, units will have different levels and quality of available inputs, and multi-purpose units can devote only a proportion of this total to anti-drugs operations. Moreover, it is not clear whether managerial decisions or individual productivity is being assessed. Faced with a fixed quantity and quality of input, managerial decisions are made about the optimal mix of processes. There is a clear difference between optimum individual productivity (doing a job to the best of one's ability), and optimum managerial decision-making (the designated job is the best use of one's time).

In addition, evaluating units on the basis of output is problematic due to the intervention of external factors over which the units may have little if any control. The extent to which units can influence the number of arrests for drugs offences is uncertain, given that many may be incidental outputs from other processes. Some units, such as designated drugs squads, should have little opportunity of making contingent arrests. The most reliable way to control for input from contingent operations may be to analyse the performance of particular units over time, and look for incremental changes over the default or minimum number of contingent arrests.

In evaluations of interventions (types (iii) to (v) listed at the beginning of this chapter), use of routine data clearly only represents an evaluation of current practice. The high failure rate of some operations may be attributable to the manner in which they were planned and organised. It is possible that a particular process is a powerful tactical approach, but deficiencies in the information used to decide when and where it is used, and the management expertise determining how it is used, explain the failure rate.

In conclusion, many factors outside of individual units' control may affect the outcome of operations, and will cause the optimal mix of police interventions to change. Evaluation of performance, and explanation of the results achieved, require a rigorous analysis and detailed understanding of how variables external to the control of the organisation are operating and influencing outcomes. Nevertheless, the volume of resources used by the police, and perceptions of a high level of drug-related harm, make the pursuit of maximum outcome from police activity through performance measurement absolutely fundamental.

3.   Monitoring drug markets and drug-related crime

Drugs markets, police interventions and drug-related problems

Police interventions are not effective unless they impact on drugs markets.
However, there are many other influences on these markets. The markets are
complex, and it is necessary to characterise the dimensions of these markets, and the
associated outcomes that result from changes in market structure. Some drug users
and some drug dealers will cause more harm to themselves and society than others,
and police detection of some drug dealers and some drug users will be more resource-
intensive than others. A police strategy aimed at maximising the reduction in drug-
related problems needs to take into account both the harm and ease of detection of
different dealers and users.

There are two fundamental aspects to illicit drugs markets: supply and demand.
These aspects are considered separately, but research indicates that many dependent
drug users support their habit by dealing, and hence it would be mistaken to consider
dealers and users as two distinct groups of individuals.

Enforcement against drugs markets will impact on many groups: those arrested for
supply or possession; those supplying or using but not arrested; potential suppliers or
users; and the customers of arrested suppliers. The direct effects of supply arrests will
include the criminal justice and other outcomes for the arrestees, any not-yet-dealers
who take their places, and the actions taken by their customers. In addition,
indirect effects may operate through changes in 'effective prices'. Drug users not
only find resources to pay for drugs, but also put time and effort into finding drugs to
purchase, and avoid detection and health problems. Hence, the 'effective price' is
generally larger than the nominal price.

If effective prices increase, drug users face a number of options: quitting drug use
altogether; changing their drug of choice; approaching treatment agencies (Dupont
and Greene, 1972; Levine et al, 1976; Moore, 1977); reducing their consumption to
minimum levels to avoid withdrawal (Roumasset and Hadreas, 1977; Moore, 1977);
opting for protracted temporary periods of abstinence (Hartnoll and Lewis, 1984;
Moore, 1977); consuming less frequently (White and Luksetich, 1983); or
continuing their present pattern of drug use at a different level of cost. Not-yet-users
may be less likely to follow a route into drug use (White and Luksetich, 1983).
Targeted efforts against the supply of certain drugs may significantly change
consumption habits, although the developments may not always be harm-reducing
to the individual or society (Gilman and Pearson, 1991; Fraser and George, 1988).

Alternatively, police may target drug-financing crimes (Roumasset and Hadreas,
1977). Benson et al (1991) concluded that an increased focus on drug crimes in the
US had the undesirable effect of increasing property crimes, both through inflating
the cost of illicit drugs, and reducing the risks of punishment for property crimes

through the redistribution of police resources. Niskanen (1992) estimated that the former effect was probably the largest.

The fact that enforcement will impact on groups other than those arrested, and that much of this impact may be indirect, means that comprehensive measurement of the effects of enforcement requires monitoring of drugs markets. Each arrest may have different direct and indirect effects on drugs markets and drug-related problems.

Dimensions of drug dealing

Lewis et al (1985) derived a hypothetical model of the London illicit heroin market. The market was characterised as a hierarchical structure, in which each tier of dealers bought and sold smaller quantities of heroin at higher prices per gram than the tier above. The Broome report adopted this structure as a basis around which to organise police drug enforcement. In this scenario, it would be sufficient to monitor only the levels of the dealers arrested, since the effects on, and reactions of, different parts of the market could be predicted from this information. However, this model has been criticised as over-simplistic (Dorn et al, 1992) and as difficult to operationalise effectively (Wright et al, 1993).

Dorn et al (1992) identified seven different types of dealing organisations. These descriptions were compared with previous studies of the operation of drugs markets, and were proposed to be broadly inclusive of previous findings. Nevertheless, even the authors themselves suggest that at the end of the research they find their typology "less satisfactory, since it cannot represent the fluid picture of the drug market which emerged" (Dorn et al, 1992, p.xiii). Given the illegality of drug dealing it is impossible to ensure representativeness in samples, and types of dealers will vary by region, subculture and level of dealing.

A more flexible and comprehensive approach may be to identify dimensions along which different dealing organisations differ, so to reflect changes in the trafficking business, and to avoid the risk of losing detail by classifying observations into discrete categories. Dimensions could be identified, and measures derived, which predicted the level of harm caused by each trafficking unit, and the likelihood and effectiveness of enforcement intervention. This may, in time, be developed into a points system. Three broad dimensions and examples of the types of factors which may be included under these headings are set out in Table 2.

The first dimension is a basic *physical description* of the type of supplier and the extent of involvement in the market. Factors included under this heading are: the number of individuals employed; the frequency of drug purchases and sales; the quantities bought and sold; and the number of customers to whom drugs are sold. Early descriptions of drugs markets concentrated on these physical characteristics.

Table 2: Dimensions of drug dealing

DIMENSION	SUB-DIMENSION
PHYSICAL –	Number employed Frequency of purchases and sales Quantities bought and sold Number of customers
PHILOSOPHY –	Allegiance to drug scene Use of violence Strength of profit-motive Level of legitimate business
CONCEALMENT –	Anti-surveillance techniques Division of drugs and money

Larger operations are likely to be more easily detected, but unless convictions can be secured against all members of the organisation, the management structure will exist to quickly replace the arrested dealer. The frequency of sales will determine both the probability of police attention, and the speed with which absence from the market will have an impact. Suppliers who deal in larger quantities and with a larger customer base have a higher probability of detection and their removal will offer the greatest reductions in drug-problems. In these terms, the logic of targeting larger scale dealers is clear – detection should be easier and the rewards of removal are more substantial.

A second dimension identified in more recent research is the *philosophy* of drug suppliers. This dimension includes: (i) strength of loyalty to the drugs scene or particular drugs, (ii) belief in retribution for deception and use of violence, (iii) the strength of the profit motive, and (iv) the intersection with legitimate business.

It is likely that those dealers with greater loyalty to the drugs scene, or particular drugs, will produce less harm, since they are likely to have better knowledge of the process, attach value to a 'good' supply of drugs, and are less likely to be reported by informers. The purity of drugs traded is important in two ways: suppliers who sell poor quality product cause more health damage through increased use of cutting agents, whilst variable levels of purity will create a greater risk of overdose. Dealers who resort to violence may be prone to detection by the police. Profit-maximisers are more likely to expand their operations and stay in business in the future, but may run a higher risk of police detection in return for higher financial rewards. Dealers with larger resources in terms of legitimate income might be expected to trade less frequently, and have less aggressive marketing policies and market practices. They are consequently less visible to the police (Dorn et al, 1992) but have more to lose from the seizure of assets.

The third dimension is the degree to which dealers exercise *concealment* to avoid detection and intervention by the police. Dorn et al (1992) describe elaborate measures to avoid police detection which may be taken by some dealers. These measures include checking of movements of police vehicles, the scanning of police radio channels, conversations with ex-policemen, and exchange of money and drugs on separate occasions. For other dealers such as 'street-sellers', visibility is desirable and an occupational hazard. Sellers react to enforcement not only by concealing involvement but also by being careful who they sell to, since they run the risk of being robbed, or selling to undercover police (White and Luksetich, 1983). Concealment from the public benefits the community and limits availability to not-yet-users. However, if drug dealers are concealed from the public they are also likely to be concealed from the police, reducing the likelihood of police intervention.

The lengths to which suppliers go to avoid police detection is the greatest predictor of the effectiveness of intelligence and surveillance work, and consequently targeted operations against selected dealers. A correlation between this dimension and the scale of dealing operations may imply that targeting 'major dealers' is not the optimal use of police resources. Better organised dealers, with more ambition to expand their enterprise and more harmful market techniques are likely to adopt the most sophisticated anti-detection and surveillance techniques. As a result, there will be an inverse relationship between the likelihood that dealers will be detected and the level of harm they cause. It may be that many operations against small-scale dealers will produce more outcome than one operation against a major dealer.

It is hoped that these dimensions will capture all the important variables which predict the level of harm caused by drug dealing and the likely impact of police anti-drug activity. There are, however, problems in quantifying the dimensions. The lack of opportunity for direct data measurement means that qualitative as well as quantitative methods may be necessary to track changes in market supply.

Dimensions of drug use

A number of variables which differentiate patterns of drug use are listed in Table 3. Drug users may have strong loyalty to specific *types of drugs*. Drug users may be described by the drugs they currently use and their potential for the use of other drugs. The type of drug(s) used will be an important determinant of the level of harm, in terms of the risks of overdose, the probability of dependence, and a propensity to violence. Poly-drug use will have hazards over and above the sum of the hazards from using the drugs independently.

Table 3: Dimensions of drug use
Types of drugs used
Frequency of use
Quantity used
Purity
Route of transmission
Relationship with dealers
Criminality
Effect sought
Price paid
Drugs expenditure

The *frequency* with which drugs are taken is one way of stratifying the drug-using population into occasional, experimental and regular drug users. Gilman and Pearson (1991) outlined five stages of drug use determined by the frequency of consumption: non-user – experimentation – occasional use on a recreational basis – 'grey area' of transitional use – habitual/compulsive/addicted use. Frequency of use reflects the level of dependence and may determine the level of interruption of the user's lifestyle, perhaps producing more harm in terms of employment, crime and the effects on the family. The stage of the drug-using career may also determine the hazard that a user will represent in terms of the risk that they will 'infect' others with a desire to use illicit drugs (Gilman and Pearson, 1991).

Just as different *stages of involvement* with drug use may imply different health education interventions (Gilman and Pearson, 1991), so will enforcement interventions be more or less effective at different stages, and transition points may be crucial. Whilst enforcement intervention may be highly effective at the experimentation stage in highlighting the implications of illicit drug use, so a large proportion of 'targets' will never graduate onto regular use (Niskanen, 1992).

Drug users may be described by the typical *quantity* of drugs they consume on a single occasion. In addition, drug users may consume different levels of drug *purity*, with some restricting their purchases to drugs of high potency (Silverman et al, 1975). The quantity used and variability in purity will affect the risk of overdose.

The degree of dependence which an individual has on drugs will determine the reaction to changes in effective prices. Dependent heroin users are likely to seek alternative sources of supply more rapidly than occasional cannabis users, although this effect may be partially mitigated by the wider availability of treatment options for heroin users.

Attention has been paid to the *route of transmission* used by different drug users, and in particular the new wave of heroin users who begin by smoking (Parker et al,

1988), and may never graduate onto injection (Griffiths et al, 1992). The level of health harm caused to the individual is linked to the route of transmission. Intravenous drug users face risks associated with poor injecting technique and the injection of impurities, as well as infectious diseases such as Hepatitis B and C, and the HIV virus, if they share equipment. The risks of overdose are reduced if drugs are smoked or ingested.

Users' behaviour will be affected by the closeness and regularity of their *relationship with their supplier* (Bean and Wilkinson, 1987). Measures taken by sellers to conceal their involvement in the drugs trade increase the search costs to users, and users face added costs of enforcement, since they may buy from undercover police or be ripped off through robbery or being sold 'a blank' (White and Luksetich, 1983). Users may seek out alternative sources of supply, but tend to buy from one or two sources, and use new sources only when they run out (Agar, 1973; Gould et al, 1974; Fiddle, 1967). Users who regularly trade with one dealer are less likely to seek alternative supplies in the short-term. In contrast, users who gain supplies from random street-traders will easily fill a gap in their drugs supply.

The closeness of the relationship between a user and any regular supplier may be an important determinant of the *typical price*, since users involved in regular trade may expect benefits in terms of reduced prices (to reflect the dealer's decreased risks of dealing with known users), as well as more flexible payment terms (Bean and Wilkinson, 1987). The response of drug use to price changes is likely to depend on the type of user involved. Silverman et al (1975) found more flexible consumption in relation to the nominal price in the short term, in users of less potent heroin, in richer neighbourhoods, and in less frequent users.

A final dimension which could be considered is the individual's propensity to criminality, with this variable perhaps reflecting job opportunities, as well as the level of criminality in the surrounding area and in the individual's peers. A combination of the average level and patterns of expenditure on drugs, and the individual's propensity to commit acquisitive crime will affect the amount of drug-related crime which may be imposed on society.

Monitoring changes in drugs markets

One way of measuring changes in drugs markets is to ask known drug users. To test the feasibility of doing this, two surveys with different methodologies were undertaken. The first involved the distribution of a one-page self-completion questionnaire in the waiting area of a Community Drug Team (CDT) on one of the GMP divisions. The second approach involved more intensive and qualitative questioning of a smaller group of drug users.

Self-completion questionnaires

The self-completion questionnaire asked respondents for details about the most recent purchase of illicit drugs they knew about (whether made by themselves or by a third party). Respondents were advised that the study aimed to investigate factors which may affect drug market conditions.

Respondents were asked to give the date on which the transaction occurred; method of payment; type of drug bought; price paid; quantity purchased; how the purity of the drug compared with the level expected; frequency with which that particular dealer is used (dealer loyalty); and area in which the transaction took place. The only question for which a significant number (N > 2) of observations were missing related to the date the transaction took place.

Thirty-eight completed questionnaires were obtained relating to sixty-two drug purchases. As shown in table 4, the majority of completed questionnaires referred to a purchase of heroin (76%), and 50% referred to a purchase of crack/cocaine. As clients of a health care agency, these respondents are not representative of Manchester drug users. Therefore, these combinations of drug purchases offer little information on current drug consumption patterns or on trends. Nevertheless, the high level of awareness of crack/cocaine purchases in this treatment-seeking group is interesting. Given the proximity of the CDT to Moss Side and Hulme, the finding that 40% of drugs were purchased in this area may not be surprising.

The mean and modal prices of drugs within this sample are shown in table 5. There is much agreement on prices, suggesting market fluctuations may appear in terms of purity. Eleven price estimates for rocks/stones of crack have been obtained. In all but two of these cases £20 per rock was paid, even when multiple rocks were purchased at one time. There were no common characteristics of the two 'high price' observations, and whilst 50% of crack purchases took place in Moss Side, purchases were made throughout Manchester.

Table 4: Combinations of drugs purchased by a sample of users, frequency with which individuals use a particular dealer, and areas in which drugs are purchased

Combinations of drugs used

	N	(%)
Heroin only	14	(37%)
Heroin and crack	9	(24%)
Crack only	5	(13%)
Heroin and cocaine	3	(8%)
Heroin and other	3	(8%)
Cocaine only	2	(5%)
Other	2	(5%)
	38	(100%)

Frequency with which individuals use that particular dealer*

	N	(%)
Always	18	(50%)
Usually	9	(25%)
Occasionally	8	(22%)
Never	1	(3%)
	36	(100%)

* Missing data in two cases

Areas in which drugs were purchased*

	N	(%)
Moss Side & Hulme	21	(40%)
Stretford	8	(15%)
Sale	7	(13%)
Wythenshawe	5	(9%)
Old Trafford	3	(6%)
Other	9	(17%)
	53	(100%)

* Missing data in 9 cases

It is possible to analyse those factors which may influence the price per unit of quantity of heroin. The majority of purchases of heroin in this sample relate to quantities of half a gram or under. There is no evidence of price discounts for bulk buys in this sample of purchases of quantities under two grams. Prices fluctuate the most in purchases of half a gram.

Table 5: Average prices paid for drugs by a sample of users analysed by relative purity, dealer loyalty and area of purchase

Average prices of drugs

Drug	Quantity	Mean	Mode	Sample size
Heroin	Gram	£45.79	£40.00	19
	Bag	£10.00	£10.00	7
Crack	Rock	£20.91	£20.00	11
Cocaine	Gram	£47.79	£50.00	4
Cannabis	1/16 Ounce	£7.50	£7.50	3
Methadone	100 ml	£9.00	–	2

Average prices per gram of heroin by level of dealer loyalty

Always use the same dealer	£43	(N=8)
Not always the same dealer	£48	(N=9)

Average prices per gram of heroin by area of purchase

Moss Side & Hulme	£50	(N=8)
Elsewhere	£42	(N=9)

Average prices per gram of heroin by realtive purity

Purity	Average price	
Less than normal	£47	(N=7)
Normal	£46	(N=8)
More than normal	£44	(N=4)

Three factors which may influence the price per gram of heroin are shown in table 5. Users who always purchase heroin from the same dealer secure a better price per gram. Analysis of this small sample of prices suggests that the Moss Side and Hulme drugs market may be the most expensive for heroin. The analysis of prices by levels of relative purity produces counter-intuitive results, with users who are most satisfied with the quality of their purchase paying the lowest prices. This result may reflect the better deal obtained by users who are most loyal to one dealer.

The self-reported relative purities of all drugs are examined in table 6. The results indicate a greater probability of customer satisfaction with the purity of drugs bought outside Moss Side and Hulme, and from a dealer who is always used. The figures are based on small samples and are unlikely to reach statistical significance, but demonstrate the potential uses of this type of data.

Table 6: Relative purity of drugs estimated by a sample of users analysed by area of purchase and dealer loyalty

Relative purity by area of purchase

	Moss Side/Hulme		Elsewhere	
	N	(%)	N	(%)
Less pure than normal	5	(28%)	6	(19%)
Normal purity	11	(61%)	18	(56%)
More pure than normal	2	(11%)	8	(25%)
	18	(100%)	32	(100%)

Relative purity by dealer loyalty

	Always the same dealer		Not always same dealer	
	N	(%)	N	(%)
Less pure than normal	2	(8%)	10	(38%)
Normal purity	13	(54%)	15	(58%)
More pure than normal	9	(38%)	1	(4%)
	24	(100%)	26	(100%)

These results indicate that the market in Moss Side and Hulme may be more likely to offer higher prices and poor quality product. This difference may reflect continued enforcement focus on the area, and higher risks faced by active dealers. Moreover, this may reflect the role of this market in offering a place of 'last resort' for users whose regular source of supply has been disrupted.

This small self-report survey of the drugs market experiences of treatment-seeking individuals demonstrates the feasibility and potential utility of this approach. Given the short study period, it is not worthwhile to look for changes over time, although this may be the major benefit of a longer study. It seems that market factors such as prices, relative purities, dealer loyalty and geographical area display significant variation which can be monitored using a self-completion questionnaire.

In-depth interviews

As an alternative method of eliciting information on the dynamics of the use and supply of heroin and crack, semi-structured interviews were held with twelve heroin users in May and June 1994. These interviews form part of the ongoing qualitative research into drug markets undertaken by the Lifeline Project in Manchester, which uses contacts with people involved in all of the drugs scenes in Manchester as a critical part of their work as a drugs advice, information and training agency.

The interviews were intended to provide insights into the organisation of the use and supply of heroin and crack in Greater Manchester in the late Spring and early Summer of 1994. The exercise was also designed to test the feasibility of using a panel of people in future to report back at intervals on changes and events in the local drugs market. Clearly, though, the sample size is not large enough to draw any conclusions concerning wider trends.

The twelve interviewees were resident in three police divisions – four in each. They were contacted through Lifeline's needle exchange scheme and all but one were consequently injecting their drugs. Most respondents were white males aged between 17 and 27 who used heroin and/or another opiate (methadone) every day. All twelve were unemployed although only nine were in receipt of social security payments (income support). The three others were solely reliant on 'alternative' sources of income including a variety of criminal activities such as shoplifting, theft from cars and begging. Only two respondents owned their own houses. Six were in council or private rented accommodation. Four were officially of 'no fixed abode' and were squatting or moving between friends' houses and flats. Of the nine respondents in receipt of social security payments only one claimed to be able to manage within this 'official' budget. The other eight were variously involved in begging, selling newspapers, thefts from shops, cars or houses and drug dealing.

The first and most striking finding was that all had used or were still using crack (known as 'rock' or 'stone') as an adjunct to their use of opiates. Respondents claimed that crack had been around in Manchester for up to three years – however, from their perspective, the last year has seen a distinct rise in its use.

For several respondents, use of crack had dominated their daily drug use at times, with opiates being used to alleviate the crack 'crash' or 'come down'. All respondents felt that the only way to keep the use of crack under any kind of control was to have access to an opiate drug, the most easily accessible opiate in Manchester being brown heroin (known simply as 'brown').

All the respondents saw the use of crack as a growing problem with the potential to dwarf the social problems traditionally associated with heroin. It was as easily available as heroin from dealers who specialised in both drugs. All respondents said they knew of "hundreds of people" who use "brown and stone" and they had immediate access to at least four sources of both heroin and crack.

Some respondents had as many as twenty telephone numbers that they said they could ring to buy heroin and crack. These drugs are available at several sites in Manchester and users will, and often do, 'shop around' various dealers. These dealers are based in different parts of Manchester, but Moss Side and Hulme are still the most often cited dealing areas. The interviews suggested that the mobile telephone has transformed the process of buying and selling heroin and crack, which was described by respondents as rapidly moving in the direction of a pizza-style home delivery service. As one respondent said:

> "When you've got the money you want the gear as soon as possible you don't want to be hanging about and the last one I had was taking half an hour...that's too long for me."

Some of those resident outside central Manchester said that, after placing the order from a phone near their homes, they would travel some way towards central Manchester to pick up their mobile telephone order of heroin or crack, crossing the boundaries of police divisions in the process.

Respondents were asked whether they had changed their dealer since last summer and most of them had, several times. The most commonly cited reasons were the 'bad attitude' of some dealers and the constant search for better 'bags' and bigger 'stones' of crack. Interestingly only one person described getting any hassle from a former dealer. Respondents normally paid £10 for a 'quarter gramme' bag of heroin which would have sold for £15 twelve months earlier. The market price of crack had fallen on occasions from £25 to £15 per rock/stone (users claim that these are roughly equivalent to 0.25 of a gramme). These reductions in price reflect the fact that there is a buyers' market with intense internal competition.

All respondents mentioned the rise in violence and intimidation associated with various drug scenes, and the general intimidation and increased use of firearms in distribution networks. This was most evident in heroin and crack markets, but several also made mention of the rise of violence on the dance drug scene in Manchester.

When asked about any policing activities that had affected their access to heroin and crack, all respondents said that there had been no significant impact over the previous twelve months. When delays were mentioned they were attributed in each case to a highly visible uniformed presence on the street following serious incidents. However, these delays were measured in minutes and hours, not days or weeks. They were a minor irritation, given the general availability of supply. Serious interruptions to supplies were said to occur at the time of Ramadan and other Muslim festivals.

All the respondents said that there was an abundance of dealers, and the competition was such that as one dealer's telephone went down, because he had been arrested or ceased trading, another number was set up immediately. Respondents spoke of dealers selling their telephone numbers and associated customers of that telephone as a going concern.

All of the respondents said that they could definitely buy heroin and crack within the hour, and for the majority the norm was 15 to 20 minutes. Ease of access is illustrated by one response to the question of how long it usually took to score heroin:

> "What time is it now? [it was 11.00 a.m.]. Well I didn't wake up till 10.00 and I've scored already...so you can see how easy it is can't you!"

Ten of the twelve respondents had been arrested since last summer. None of them had been given an arrest referral card. None of the respondents thought that the police had changed their policies towards drug users since last summer. All the users who had been arrested were highly critical of the police surgeons because of their alleged punitive attitudes.

Respondents saw methadone as a pure substitute for heroin. Where the access existed, it provided them with an alternative for which they were grateful on occasions. Five respondents had bought it over the previous month, but all of these were very wary of it and concerned about its addictive potential. Ironically, these respondents saw heroin as the safer drug. Living with the ever present threat of imprisonment, these interviewees were emphatic that they would much prefer to start a prison sentence with a heroin, rather than a methadone, habit. For some respondents, methadone had provided the means of 'returning to a normal life', and relief from engaging in crime which they had detested. All respondents suggested that the price of illegally purchased methadone linctus is £1 for 10ml; a market price which has remained constant in Manchester for almost ten years. Discounts are available if people are prepared to buy methadone in bulk.

Qualitative in-depth interviews with drug users do provide a useful additional source of information. It would be feasible for independent agencies such as Lifeline to be commissioned to construct representative panels of different types of drug users for this purpose. The major benefit of this exercise would be the monitoring of changes in the market over time.

Drug use and crime – review

Crime and illicit drug use are linked in a number of ways. Drug use and trafficking are, of course, crimes in themselves. Users, however, may be more likely to commit other offences and some offences will be directly linked to financing the habit. Crime may also result from association with the drug culture, through disputes over use or supply. Encounters between people buying and selling drugs may lead to other types of offences. Finally, drugs affect mood and personality, and crime may be committed whilst under the influence of these drugs. Responding to this diversity, analysis carried out to explore the drugs-crime relationship includes studies of the criminal careers of drug users, of the drug use of those who have committed crimes, and micro-economic studies of the incomes and expenditures of drug users.

Criminal careers of drug users

The bulk of drugs-crime literature analyses the criminal histories of illicit drug users. There are four potential groups of this population:

(i)   drug users who have never committed non-drug crimes;

(ii)   drug users who begin to commit non-drug crimes after starting drug use;

(iii) drug users who committed non-drug crimes before they started using drugs, and do not increase their rate of offending;

(iv)   drug users who committed non-drug crimes before they started using drugs, but the rate at which they commit non-drug crimes increases.

There are widely differing estimates of the size of group (i). In Mott's (1981) analysis of the Home Office Addicts Index, 20-30% of males and 40-50% of females had never been convicted of an offence before becoming notified. Only 13% of Jarvis and Parker's (1989) sample, however, had not committed a crime in the six months before entering prison or treatment where they were contacted for the study.

Fazey (1991) estimated that one-quarter of heroin users would fit into group (ii). Based on 61 interviews with known heroin users, Parker et al (1988) estimated that 42% of known heroin users committed no crime before their heroin use, but began resorting to acquisitive crime afterwards. The comparable percentage from Jarvis and Parker's (1989) study is 27%. The majority of problem users contacted in studies by Burr (1987), Parker et al (1988), and Jarvis and Parker (1989), would be classified into group (iv). Significantly, Burr (1987) found no evidence that the rate of offending would decrease if there was a reduction in illicit heroin use.

Perhaps the greatest difference between drug-using and non-drug using offenders is in the types of crime committed. Mott's (1981) review of the Home Office Addicts Index revealed that for both males and females, non-drug offences were usually theft. Violent crimes and prostitution were rare at that time. Similarly, a later Home Office Statistical Department study (1985) found that the proportion of first convictions for personal violence was 6% in male notified addicts, in comparison to a rate of 12% in the general convicted population.

Drug use by criminals

An alternative way to investigate the drugs-crime relationship is to assess the extent of criminals' drug use. Mott (1991) suggests that few individuals in the criminal underworld in the 1970s were drug users. The role played by drugs in national crime levels was investigated in a Home Office Statistical Department (1985) survey, which found that only 4% of notifiable offences recorded by the police during the period 1979 to 1982 were committed by notified addicts.

However, where local epidemics of drug use occur, the impact may be large. Mott (1986) found that 20% of individuals convicted of residential burglaries in the Wirral in 1983 were notified addicts, compared to a national average of 3-11%. Parker and Newcombe (1987) found that, in a sample of individuals convicted of burglary, 50% were known problem heroin users compared to only 4% convicted of criminal damage.

Financing a drug habit

Assessing the pressure which a regular drug habit puts on the income of an average drug user may further illuminate the links between drugs and crime. The rate of unemployment in individuals seeking help for drug problems is notoriously high, and drug dealing may be the major alternative source of finance. Collison (1993) suggested that 60% of clients at the local Community Drug Team financed their drug use through drug supply, burglary or shoplifting. Equally, in Parker et al's (1988) sample, only 26% financed their problem heroin use through legal means or drug dealing and Jarvis and Parker's (1989) study of problem opiate users found only 28% managing to finance a heroin habit without resorting to non-drug crimes.

Conclusion

Mott (1981) identified five important factors which affected the results obtained in surveys of drugs and crime: (i) the selection of groups; (ii) the stage of drug-using career; (iii) the proportion of observations from each sex; (iv) the country of birth; and (v) the length of follow-up period. Results may say more about the criteria used to select study entrants than the drugs-crime relationship. Findings which disregard these factors should be treated with caution.

These factors demonstrate the problem in identifying representative relationships between drugs and crime. In particular, the use of the Home Office Addicts Index as a register of drug users is problematic, given the small subset of regular opiate users that this register includes, and the particular types of users which may be represented (such as older, more dependent users). Although the use of convictions as the sole measure of the number of offences committed is likely to be somewhat inaccurate and biased, the research shows drug-using offenders to be more likely than non drug-using offenders to be apprehended for non-drug offences, and notified users to be more likely to have a conviction than non-notified users.

Changes in drug use will not affect these different types of relationships equally and this complicates the development of objective indicators. Although a fall in drug use may lead to a reduction in possession offences, because of these other relationships, drug-related other offences may not fall by the same amount. For example, the user who was committing crime before drug use, even if now abstaining, may only reduce his criminal activity to previous levels, or may not reduce it at all. It is also possible that, being in a better physical state, he may actually increase it, but spend his gains elsewhere than on illicit drugs.

For these reasons, it is important to emphasise that the intersection of drug-using and criminal behaviours does not prove a **causal** linkage between them. The pressures of financing a drug habit or committing crime may be considerable for a number of reasons, some of which may be connected with the lifestyle of those involved (Walters, 1994). So, although a correlation between crime and drugs misuse can be shown and a reduction in crime may intuitively be expected if level of drugs misuse and expenditure on drugs is reduced, there is no mechanism through which we can strictly predict and quantify the extent of that reduction.

The drugs-crime connection continues to fuel debate and controversy in the drugs literature and elsewhere. The statistics cited earlier have been subjected to a good deal of critical scrutiny and accused of "over-dramatisation" (Ramsay, 1994). The precise nature of the connection is only likely to be established after more research and even then, if the debate about the alcohol and crime connection is any guide, the question may remain unanswered.

Survey of divisional arresting officers

It was decided, because of these difficulties, to investigate some aspects of the drug-crime connection from the point of view of arresting officers, using arrests as the starting point. There were several reasons for this. Firstly, a survey would provide base-line data on the proportion of people arrested in three months of 1994, who were perceived to have a drugs problem. This would enable a comparison to be made at some future date if the survey was repeated. Secondly, assuming other things remained equal, a reduction in the proportion of drug abusers among those arrested later, might be taken as evidence that the strategy was beginning to have an effect. If the instrument proved to be robust, and if the response rate was good, it could be used as the basis for a composite performance indicator. Thirdly, if the force was to adopt a more selective referral system in future, then data collected on drugs connections might provide a quick way of identifying those who should be targeted.

The findings of the survey were also intended to contribute to the debate about the drugs-crime connection. In this context, the findings need to be approached with caution. The data relate to people who were arrested on *suspicion* of committing the stated offences. Some of them would subsequently not have been charged and some would have been found not-guilty at court. The analysis of the drugs-crime connection discussed below relates to the proportion of those who came to attention because they were arrested and whose apparent drug involvement was discovered by the arresting officer.

The survey was designed to examine the officers' reasons for stating that there was evidence of drug abuse. Indicators of drugs involvement included possession of drugs, possession of drugs-using or drugs-dealing equipment, previous drugs convictions, requests for medication whilst in custody etc. Officers on B,C and M divisions were asked to complete a questionnaire on each arrest made during January, February and March 1994. 6174 arrests were made in that period and 4109 questionnaires were returned, making a response rate of 67%. Summary tables are included in the tables 7 to 9.

The offences investigated

The 4109 completed questionnaires covered a wide range of offences. Theft was the offence for which the greatest number of people were arrested (21%), followed by wanted-on-warrant (11%), burglary (8%), assault occasioning actual bodily harm (5%) and breach of the peace (5%). No other offence-code reached 5% of the sample. For the purposes of the analysis, the offences charged were aggregated into eighteen categories. Theft (which includes theft of and from vehicles which could not be analysed separately, as the data was derived from charge sheets, rather than reported crime), was the largest category, followed by a group of offences including courts-related procedures (warrants, etc) and traffic offences. 187 drugs offences were identified (5% of the sample).

Levels of drugs connections

755 cases (19% of the overall sample) were found to have some drugs connection. The most frequently cited indicator of a drugs connection was a previous conviction for a drugs offence (73% of cases where a connection was cited); followed by drugs related items found at home or at work (21%); admission made that the crime was committed to finance a drug habit (21%); and drugs-related items found on the person at the time of arrest (16%). A variety of other reasons given by officers for believing there was a connection were categorised together in a miscellaneous category (31%). No other category reached the level of 3% of the sample. Because some officers could cite more than one reason in their answers, the above percentages do not total 100%. A breakdown is shown in table 7; percentages in the table relate to the total 4109 questionnaires returned. The 187 offences where drugs were the single specific reason for the arrest are not included in this analysis.

Table 7: Drugs-involvement indicators

Involvement indicator (n = 4109)	(n)	%
*Previous conviction offence	(552)	13%
Other drugs/crime connection known to officer	(226)	6%
*Drugs-related items found at home or work address	(161)	4%
*Detained person known to police as an addict	(161)	4%
*Admission made at police station that crime committed to finance drugs	(142)	3%
*Drug-related items found on person at time of arrest	(117)	3%
Drugs found on person at time of arrest	(88)	2%
*Detainee requested medication whilst in custody	(67)	2%
*Drugs found at home or at work address	(64)	2%
*Admission made at court that crime committed to	(36)	<1%

To provide a better and more integrated measure of the drugs-crime connection, a new variable was computed which combined the individual factors indicating drugs involvement. Specific drugs offences were again excluded. Using this composite variable, the drugs-crime connection proved to be stronger for some offence types than others (table 8), although it should be noted that some offence categories contained very small numbers of cases. Firearms offences were most significantly related to drugs involvement (53%) followed by burglary (31%), very serious offences such as murder, and robbery offences (30% each), offences involving courts procedures (26%), sexual offences, including prostitution (23%), theft (21%), criminal attempts and conspiracy (20%), fraud (20%), autocrime (19%), detention under the Police and Criminal Evidence Act (17%), public order offences (12%), traffic offences (11%), offences of personal violence (11%), licensing offences, mainly drunkenness (10%) and criminal damage (9%).

Table 8: Drugs connection found by crime type

Offence-type (n = 4109)	% drugs involved	% drugs not involved	All cases %	(n)
*Firearms offences	53.3	46.7	100.0	(15)
*Burglary: including burglary with intent, aggrevated burglary	31.3	68.7	100.0	(342)
Very serious offences: murder abduction, blackmail, etc	30.0	70.0	100.0	(20)
*Robbery: including assult with intent to rob, attempted robbery	30.0	70.0	100.0	(140)
*Courts offences: including perverting justice, bail offences warrants	26.2	73.8	100.0	(539)
Sexual offences: including rape, indecency, prostitution	23.2	76.8	100.0	(125)
Theft: including theft of/ from motor vehicles	21.3	78.7	100.0	(875)
Conspiracy and attempts not included in other categories	20.0	80.0	100.0	(5)
Fraud: criminal deception forgery, etc	19.7	80.3	100.0	(137)
Autocrime: taking vehicle without consent, etc	19.0	81.0	100.0	(284)
PACE detentions	17.0	83.0	100.0	(94)
*Public order: including affray, Public Order Act, breach of peace	12.4	87.6	100.0	(380)
*Traffic/highways: including B-tests, disqualified drivers	11.5	88.5	100.0	(407)
*Personal violence: GBH, ABH assaults, offensive weapon, etc	11.1	88.9	100.9	(305)
*Licensing offences: drunkeness, etc	10.0	90.0	100.0	(70)
Damage offences: criminal damage, arson, hoaxes/threats, etc	9.2	90.8	100.0	(207)
Aliens and immigration	–	100.0	100.0	(5)

Table 9: Drugs connection found by crime type where premises had been searched by police

Offence-type (n = 868)	% drugs involved	% drugs not involved	All cases %	(n)
*Courts offences: including perverting justice, bail offences warrants	74.5	25.5	100.0	(55)
Firearms offences	62.5	37.5	100.0	(8)
Traffic/highways: B-tests, disqualified drivers	57.1	42.9	100.0	(14)
Robbery: including assault with intent to rob and attempted robbery	47.4	52.6	100.0	(57)
Public order: including affray, Public Order Act, breach of peace	44.4	55.6	100.0	(18)
Burglary: including burglary with intent and aggravated burglary	42.2	57.8	100.0	(166)
Very serious offences: murder abduction, blackmail, etc	38.5	61.5	100.0	(13)
Fraud: criminal deception forgery, etc	36.6	63.4	100.0	(41)
*Theft: including theft of/ from motor vehicles	29.6	70.4	100.0	(284)
Damage offences: criminal damage, arson, hoaxes/threats, etc	29.4	70.6	100.0	(17)
PACE detentions	28.6	71.4	100.0	(7)
*Personal violence: GBH, ABH assaults, offensive weapon, etc	27.8	72.2	100.0	(36)
Autocrime: taking vehicle without consent, etc	26.6	73.4	100.0	(64)
Sexual offences: indecency, rape, prostitution, etc	16.7	83.3	100.0	(12)
Conspiracy and attempts not included in other categories	0.0	100.0	100.0	(2)
*Licensing offences: drunkeness, etc	0.0	100.0	100.0	(1)
Aliens and immigration	0.0	100.0	100.0	(1)

Drugs-crime involvement and police searches

Viewed in the context of previous claims about the connection between drugs and crime, the proportion of drugs related offences was lower than had been expected, particularly for acquisitive crimes such as burglary, robbery and theft. We thought that one explanation might be that we were measuring the effect of police searching practices. If an arresting officer does not search the arrested person's premises, there may be less chance of a drugs connection being discovered.

This proved to be correct. All arrests where the officer had searched the person's premises (21% of those examined), were analysed against the offence-types previously used in Table 8. Table 9 shows the results. Comparison between these tables shows that in most cases, the disclosed levels of drugs-involvement were higher when premises were searched by police. In burglary cases it rose from 31% to 42%, in theft from 21% to 30%, in autocrime from 19% to 27%. This is largely in line with previous research. For courts offences, it rose from 26% to 74%, possibly brought about by cases where the original offence for which further court proceedings such as arrest warrants were instituted involved drugs.

Conclusions

These findings are broadly in line with previous research and lend some support to the selective targeting of police drugs referral schemes upon the offence-categories most likely to be drugs-connected. Although the findings do not indicate that the vast majority of acquisitive crime is drugs-related, the levels are substantial enough, given the gross reported figures for these offences.

The decision to search an arrested person's premises had an effect on the perceived level of the drugs-crime connection. An increase in the number of searches by arresting officers, and training for arresting officers in searching for drugs connections, would probably produce a corresponding increase in the number of cases where a drugs connection was revealed.

The approach we have used could provide a useful technique for monitoring the drugs-crime connection, using the indicators illustrated in table 7, namely:

- whether the arrested person had a conviction for a drugs offence;
- whether drugs or drugs-related items had been found on their person or in their home or work premises at the time of their arrest;
- whether they requested any medication; and
- whether they made any admission at the police station, or subsequently at court that the offence for which they had been arrested had been committed to finance a drugs habit.

An important additional piece of information which was not collected as part of this study but which would greatly help in the interpretation of these indicators would be type of drug found or used by the arrestee. If dependency on drugs such as heroin is more likely to require financing through acquisitive crime than the use of drugs such as cannabis, the type of drug used by these arrestees would have implications for the nature of the drugs-crime connection revealed by these indicators.

Although survey methods could be used, routine data collection at the time of arrest would be preferable. This would be easier once custody records were fully computerised. A computerised custody database could include fields for the indicators we have used, although further testing will be necessary. The means for measuring any change in levels over time could be provided as part of the system.

4. Diversion strategies

Diversion strategies, which may form part of a balanced drugs strategy, are an attempt to divert (some types of) drug users away from crime and the criminal justice system, into contact with the health and social care sector. Alternatively, encouragement of contact with treatment agencies may occur at later stages of the criminal justice process, under the remit of the probation or prison services. Given that health and social care agency programmes may reduce the level of drug-related harm caused to individuals and the community, police activities which encourage entry into treatment may be one way of reducing drug problems.

Effective interventions of this sort require good interaction between the criminal justice system and health and social care agencies. The attitudes of health care purchasers and the practices of providers will determine the impact of any diversion scheme. To investigate the success of these schemes through the development of objective indicators, it is necessary to understand how the care sector works. As an example of a diversion strategy intervention, this section is focused on the arrest referral scheme introduced by GMP.

Indicators may reflect the impact of activities at three levels: process, output and outcome. Process includes the implementation of the scheme in the police sector, and entry into treatment in the health and social care sector. Measures of output reflect the immediate results of the scheme, such as the additional numbers going forward for treatment. Improvements in outcome will be measured as the reduction in crime and other individual or social harms. This section includes descriptions of the process involved in implementing the scheme, through interviews with custody officers and care agency personnel. An evaluation of the output produced on one division during the first six months of the scheme is summarised later in this section, and the likely impact of the encouragement of drug users into treatment on levels of outcome discussed.

Process in the police sector: a survey of custody officers

The force strategy requires custody officers to ensure that every person coming into custody, irrespective of the offence for which they were arrested, is handed a referral card. Not everyone handed a card will accept it. The referral cards provide a list of the names and addresses of local agencies which can assist people who have a drugs problem. This referral scheme is founded on the assumption that the receipt of the card will persuade people to present themselves at one of the health or social care agencies. If this assumption is correct, then custody officers are one of the key determinants of the effectiveness of this part of the strategy. In the same way that officers may not search premises and hence fail to discover a drugs-crime connection, custody officers may prevent someone seeking aid by withholding the referral card. Their role is an example of the key intervening variables which shape outputs. We shall refer to these factors later in the conclusion to the report and suggest that performance evaluation must take account of them and, if possible, measure their effect. The survey of custody officers was designed to be a step in this direction.

The sample

Every custody office in the Force area was visited on two occasions and the custody officer on duty at the time was interviewed. Every effort was made to ensure randomness in sampling. 56 custody officers were interviewed (48% of the total). These interviews concentrated on their knowledge of, and attitudes towards, the strategy, the training they had received, and their workload. The majority (59%) had in excess of 15 years service and 16% had less than 10 years service. 52% had less than 5 years in the rank with the remaining 48% having 5 years or more. 61% had been custody officers for less than 12 months. 11% had held the position for between 1 and 2 years and the remaining 27% for more than 2 years.

Results

The average number of prisoners dealt with during the period of analsis was 161 per officer (officers included both custody officers and clerks). Most custody officers (70%) equated the strategy with the referral system and two thirds stated they were not fully conversant with it. 55% viewed the referral scheme positively themselves but only 7% believed that arresting officers viewed the scheme positively. Only 11% thought senior officers held a positive attitude to the scheme. 64% believed the scheme was viewed negatively by persons coming into custody. A positive attitude towards the scheme from the custody officer could be instrumental in optimising the take up rate.

The survey indicates that cards were not being issued to every arrested person. Only 18% of the sample stated that they issued cards to every prisoner. Half of those who were selective decided on the basis of the offence, 24% on the prisoner's appearance, 15% on whether or not the detainee appeared to want help, 9% on admissions of dependency and 2% on previous convictions.

Only 18% of custody officers indicated that they had received any training about the strategy and 61% of these considered that training would be beneficial. It is perhaps not surprising to find that training is important. 80% of those who had been trained held a positive attitude. The data suggest that training has a significant effect on the attitudes of the longer service group and it is they who should be targeted. However training, whilst improving attitudes, has so far not had a significant effect on enhancing the custody officers' knowledge of the strategy. It is worthy of note that there is a positive correlation between knowledge of the strategy and a positive attitude amongst those custody officers with 15 years or less service. This again reinforces the argument that the target group for training and expanding knowledge should be those officers with more than 15 years service.

Analysis of the data provides a number of points of interest. Attitude to the scheme does not appear to be significantly affected by factors such as workload, location or length of service. This is a very useful finding, as from the outset it was hoped that attitudes could be modified by factors which lie within the control of the organisation. Training is the sole factor which has a significant effect on attitude and the results have pointed to the group for whom training proves most effective.

Process in the health and social care sector: a survey of care agency personnel

There are many routes into the health and social care sector for drug misusers (see Figure 2). Individuals frequently use the different services currently provided simultaneously, and there is little evidence of a clear route through this sector which relates to case-severity. The philosophies of programmes vary, some based on detoxification and abstinence, some focused on reducing drug use, and others providing prescription of substitute drugs. The number of drug users in contact with treatment agencies is a small proportion of those who may benefit. Available evidence on expected outcomes from treatment, including reductions in criminal behaviour, is reviewed later in this section.

The sample

Seventeen interviews were undertaken between January and May 1994 with, primarily, managers of health and/or social care agencies in the Greater Manchester area. Eleven of these interviews were with Community Drug Team (CDT) Managers, the remainder representing the network of needle/syringe exchange schemes, a non-statutory advice and counselling service, the Greater Manchester Probation Service, a non-statutory service for drug-misusing probation clients, and a service for people with HIV/AIDS. Interviewees were questioned about the nature of their service, origins of referral, significant influences on their work, outcome assessment, the availability of data, and their perceptions of the GMP Drugs Misuse Strategy.

Service provision

The nature and range of services provided by CDTs varied considerably. The maximum dose of methadone per day which the team was prepared to prescribe varied from 60ml – 120ml, and a few prescribed amphetamine substitutes. Of the eleven CDTs, six did not have a waiting list currently and four had short waiting lists (4-5 weeks). It was suggested that details of waiting times permeate the drug-using community, and drug users tend to be fairly impatient clients, whose resolve to enter treatment does not persist. The role of waiting time was sufficiently important in

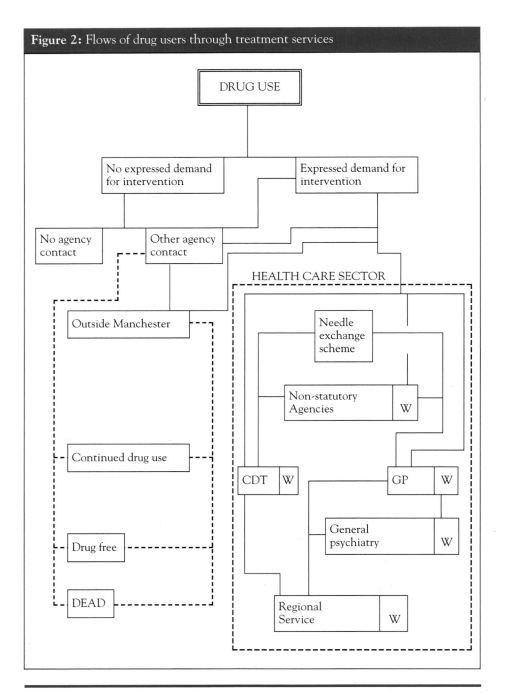

Figure 2: Flows of drug users through treatment services

one case to be written into the contract with the purchaser as a quality measure. On the other hand, it was suggested that, for those already receiving treatment, waiting lists may have a beneficial effect since they are less likely to drop out of contact.

In general, whilst it was suspected that other factors, such as enforcement agency activity and drug market conditions, were potential influences on activity, little firm evidence was provided. Seasonal fluctuations in numbers self-referring for treatment during Ramadan and at the start of the calendar year were reported. Where drug market conditions fluctuated, it was thought that shortages would affect demand for services and the rate at which existing clients attended appointments.

Outcomes to which CDT services were oriented included: criminal activity and illicit drug use; HIV and injection; general health status; and relationships, employment, and abstinence from/reduction of all drug use. The prominence of reductions in criminal activity is interesting. Given this level of agreement between the police and other agencies about preferred outcomes, it is a pity that police initiatives to coerce increasing numbers of drug users into treatment will be difficult to monitor, since not all client contacts are recorded, and there is variation between agencies in what is recorded, most importantly, in terms of source of the referral (police or other). Furthermore, data are not currently collected which would allow an assessment of the extent to which additional users coerced into treatment represent improvements in societal outcome.

Perceptions of the GMP drugs misuse strategy

In general, the objectives of the new strategy were believed to be the reduction of drug-related crimes, the encouragement of more drug-users into treatment and saving police resources. The elements of the strategy that were widely recognised were the arrest referral scheme, lobbying for the increased availability of substitute drugs and increased multi-agency work.

The overall assessment of the strategy was one of cautious approval. Particular shortcomings expressed were (the misguided view) that the new cautioning policy should not have been confined to possession offences – in certain circumstances more serious offences qualify for a caution – that the strategy ignored crack cocaine and other drugs, and that there was little compulsion for users to enter treatment. Furthermore, many drug-using offenders would not be involved with the criminal justice system for drugs offences, so the cautioning initiative would have little effect. It was noted that the success of the arrest referral scheme would depend on the extent to which treatment agencies were already in contact with the majority of problem drug users in the area.

Many thought that the alleged strength of the relationship between drugs and crime on which the strategy was based was over-stated and over-simplified. In general, favourable comments were made about the major philosophical change that the strategy implied, which was interpreted as a focus away from prosecution and a recognition that enforcement alone could not work. The strongest reservations about the strategy were that the police did not have the interests of drug users at heart. It was suggested that initiatives should have been introduced to improve the availability of methadone in custody, and resources for expanded treatment services should have accompanied the proposals. Moreover, there was scepticism about whether the strategy would actually be implemented, since there was evidence that arrest referral cards were not being handed out, and that the opinions of lower ranking officers had not changed.

An output evaluation of the arrest referral scheme

Method

The output evaluation involved a comparison of the numbers self-referring for treatment before and after the introduction of the scheme. However, a simple comparison of total numbers offers no advice on why the scheme does or does not work, or allow for other factors which may explain differential rates over time, such as treatment capacity, waiting lists, changing characteristics and size of the drug-using population, changing treatment protocols, and drug-market conditions (Kay, undated).

Fortunately, two recent advances in information technology in the Manchester area enabled a more sophisticated approach in this project. First, a computerised register of all arrests, including details of the person arrested, means of disposal in the case, and offences committed, has been operational in one division of the Greater Manchester Police since April 1993. Second, the North Western Regional Health Authority has the longest running Regional Drug Misuse Database in the country. The automation of the collection of these data provides a useful opportunity for their cost-effective, routine comparison.

The Regional Drug Misuse Database receives 'attributor' information from treatment agencies on new client contacts or contacts by former clients who have not been in contact in the previous six months. The 'attributors' used to distinguish between records are first and surname initials, dates of birth and sex. This information is required to calculate the number of persons known to the database as opposed to the number of contact-events, since people may contact multiple agencies or have several contacts with the same agency separated by periods longer than six months.

Matching of the files from the police and drug misuse databases could produce confidentiality and ethical dilemmas. A system was devised which ensured the confidentiality of cases and which may be useful for the police to adopt in further research which involves the transfer of arrestee details to third parties.

The proposed plan was that the names of arrested persons would be coded as first and surname initials and a sex variable, and that a simplified version of this file, containing types of offence, ethnic origin, and date of arrest, would be passed to the Regional Health Authority's Drug Research Unit. The Drug Research Unit would add details of any pre or post-arrest contacts with treatment agencies which are close to the arrest date, including details such as drug(s) used, planned treatment etc. The extended file would be returned to the researchers with attributors removed, and other variables such as dates of birth and date of arrest recoded, such that individuals could not be identified from the original police arrest file.

This approach allows many issues to be addressed. The data could be divided by month of arrest to identify whether the scheme was having a gradually increasing impact, rather than an immediate impact on the date of introduction. The role of police arrest in creating a 'point of crisis' at which an individual may seek treatment could be examined, by analysing the time-gap between arrest and contact. In addition, the probability that an arrestee will seek treatment could be studied depending on whether they received a charge, caution or release without charge, and the offence for which they were arrested.

In the event, however, there was insufficient time for these analyses within the time-scale of this project because of perceived problems with the Data Protection Act. Therefore, a less ambitious, and more aggregate analysis was undertaken, which demonstrated the feasibility of using these data. The police arrest file was divided into two time frames: before and after the introduction of the scheme. The two data sets were initially matched with the agency information for the same six-month periods. The number of arrestees who had contacted a CDT or GP after the date of their arrest was counted. In addition, contacts with any of these agencies in the six-months prior to the date of arrest were noted, since this may be a good indication that an individual was already in contact with an agency, and was therefore not a target for the scheme.

Results

In the six-month period prior to the setting-up of the referral scheme (1/4/93 – 30/9/93), 3363 individuals were arrested on this sub-division. In the six-month period following the introduction of the scheme (1/10/93 – 31/3/94), 3555 individuals were arrested and dealt with on the same sub-division. The percentages and numbers who made contact with CDTs or GPs in the six-months prior to their arrest, and/or following their arrest within the study period, are given in Table 10.

The finding that over 1% of the arrested sample made contact in a short period after their arrest indicates the importance of police arrest as a potential influence on self-referral. These 76 persons are likely to represent a large proportion of the arrestees who have a drug problem and could benefit from treatment. The percentages making contact before or after the date of arrest are not comparable due to assymetries in the time periods concerned. For example, for an individual arrested on 4th January 1994, the six-month period prior to arrest (4/7/93 – 3/1/94) is analysed for contacts with agencies, whereas a shorter period (4/1/94 – 31/3/94) is analysed for post-arrest contacts.

Table 10: Pre and post-arrest agency contacts, before and during the scheme				
Type of contact	Before the scheme		During the scheme	
	%	(n)	%	(n)
Contact after arrest, and no contact in previous six months	1.13	(37)[1]	0.92	(32)
Contact after arrest, and contact in previous six months	0.12	(4)[1]	0.09	(3)[1]
Total contact after arrest	1.26	(41)[1]	1.01	(35)[1]
No contact after arrest, but contact in previous six months	2.94	(99)	2.36	(84)
Total arrestees		(3363)		(3555)

[1] Percentages based on total arrestees minus those who had no contact after arrest, but contact in the previous six months, and were therefore not targets for the scheme.

Table 10 reveals that the percentage of potential targets for the scheme (see footnote to table 10) who made contact with an agency actually fell slightly after the introduction of the scheme (from 1.3% to 1.0%). The fact that almost 3% of the arrestees were already in contact with agencies demonstrates the importance of allowing for this group when evaluating arrest referral schemes. These data should, however, be interpreted with caution. It may be that fewer drug users have attempted or been able to make contact with these agencies in the latter period because of the re-organisation of services or longer waiting times. Alternatively, this decrease may be linked to police process, including a different time distribution of arrests between the two periods (ie. arrestees in the former sample may have had more time to contact agencies if a greater proportion were arrested in the early part of the period). In addition, the police may have arrested fewer drug-misusing offenders, and/or drug-misusing offenders who were less likely to seek treatment.

Based on the results of previous evaluations of arrest referral schemes for drugs, these findings may not be surprising (Dorn, 1994). In Southwark, over a 25-month period only 0.4% of arrestees were recorded as taking up the chance of referral, with the take-up rate still below 1% in persons arrested for possession offences (Southwark Arrest Referral Scheme Evaluation, undated). Only in the case of trafficking offences did a significant percentage respond (14%).

These results demonstrate the utility of comparing police arrest and Drug Misuse Database files. It is clear that further analysis, in the form originally planned and over a longer time period, is required for the effective evaluation of the GMP Arrest Referral Scheme. However, an output indicator which can be used for the evaluation of police arrest activity has been derived and demonstrated.

Expected outcomes of diversion strategies

Abstinence-based and drug-reducing regimes

Just as evaluations of the effectiveness of policing in terms of rehabilitating offenders and reducing re-offending have been disappointing (Pearson, 1990), so have treatment evaluations in terms of abstinence from drug use. Many drug users will quit using drugs at some stage and it is difficult to determine the role of treatment in this process. The literature suggests that those who do not receive treatment are just as likely to 'recover' from drug use, although non-treated ex-drug users feel that treatment would have been useful at the time of withdrawal (Watson, 1985).

A significant shift towards negative testimonies about a drug-using career and a denial of any pleasure from drug use may be necessary for complete abstinence (Gilman and Pearson, 1991). 'Getting off and staying off' may depend on a change in the drug user's social and economic environment, as much as available treatment (Whynes, 1991).

If the motivation for seeking treatment is not abstinence but a recognition of persistent problems relating to drug use, or a reluctance to continue bearing the risks and costs of illicit drug use, the most appropriate solution may be the stable supply of substitute drugs. As such, treatment may reduce many of the problems associated with the intravenous consumption of street drugs and the need to pay illicit market prices.

A further reason for entry to treatment is the coercion of the authorities and Courts. The motivation to quit in this group is likely to be lower, and the only problems which may be clearly associated with drug use in the user's mind may be legal problems. This situation suggests traditional drug treatments may not be as effective in terms of achieving abstinence or reducing non-crime measures of drug-related harm, since personal motivation is likely to be a significant determinant of treatment effectiveness (Rounsaville and Kleber, 1985).

UK studies do not tend to divide evaluations of drug treatments by the reason for entering treatment. US studies suggest that patients whose sentences contain an element of coercion into treatment derive similar benefits to voluntary entrants in terms of reductions in illicit drug use and property crime (Brecht, Anglin and Wang, 1993). However, the coerced group in this study were brought into treatment later, rather than earlier, in their drug-using career.

Methadone maintenance

Several studies have been undertaken of the potential for prescribing regimes to reduce illicit drug use. Thorley's (1987) review of British longitudinal studies concluded that only one-third of clients were abstinent after five years, which was a disappointing result in reference to the 'success' of methadone maintenance in the US in the 1960s. A more integrated system including clinics, Community Drug Teams, rehabilitation houses and self-help groups in Manchester, however, was thought to have been more effective (Strang, 1989).

Surveys of drug users in treatment reveal that, at least initially, use of street drugs continues, although the quantities used and frequency of use decline significantly, by about 50% after one year (Bennett and Wright, 1986; Fazey, 1988). In tandem, the need to commit drug-financing crimes or crimes to obtain pharmaceutical supplies also decreases once users enter treatment (Fazey, 1988; Jarvis and Parker, 1988). Maintenance prescribing of oral methadone offers a way of reducing the risks from intravenous drug use, and a stable supply may reduce the tendency for overdoses.

Several large-scale US studies find that substantial improvements in behaviour accompany methadone maintenance (Senay, 1985). Ball and Ross' (1991) study of the changes in criminal activity in those entering and remaining in methadone maintenance treatment suggests impressive crime reductions can result. Comparing different cohorts, the numbers of days per year involved in crime falls from 238 in the last period of addiction, to 69 at admission, 28 after one year, and 21 after 2 years, rising slightly after this time. Forty-eight of the 126 admissions during the study period stayed in treatment for a year or more. In this sub-sample, the percentages committing crime fell from 77% during the last period of addiction, to 50% in the summer prior to admission, to 35% at the point of admission, and further to 25% after one year in treatment.

It is not clear, however, whether reductions in crime, such as the 79% in the Ball and Ross (1991) study, can be attributed to the effectiveness of methadone maintenance treatment, or a simultaneous decision on the part of the drug user to attempt to reduce illicit drug use and criminal activity. The greatest reductions in crime occur in the periods before treatment entry, and may be partly attributable to entry into other treatment facilities or prison sentences (Ball and Ross, 1991). Furthermore, length of stay and methadone dose were not found to affect criminality. Moreover, it is not clear from this study which drug users may be expected to benefit most from treatment, or whether drug users encouraged into treatment at earlier stages in their drug-using career would achieve the same reductions in criminality.

Despite the expected preference of treatment-seeking heroin users for a prescription of injectable heroin rather than an oral dose of the heroin-substitute methadone, the only controlled trial comparing the two regimes in the UK found little difference in effectiveness for those who remained in treatment (Hartnoll et al, 1980). However, whilst 74% of the group receiving injectable heroin were still in contact after 12 months, only 29% of the oral methadone group were in contact. Of the methadone non-attenders, 40% were no longer using opiates regularly. Therefore, whilst offering methadone at this time (1972-1975) reduced drug use for some, it also led to a greater population out of contact with services. In this small group, 12% of the injectable heroin group sold their prescriptions illicitly at some time.

Assessments of the role of treatment programmes should also consider negative aspects which may arise from treatment programmes. The prescription of methadone increases the number of options available to self-referred drug users at a time when they may be considering the wisdom of their drug use. It is feasible that some potential abstainers are maintained as drug addicts, albeit of legally supplied drugs. The increased availability of opiates in the community through illicit market sales of prescribed drugs may provide a cheap supply at a time when drug users may be contemplating a break from their drug-using routine. Unsupervised use of methadone in conjunction with other intoxicants can result in overdose (Senay, 1985). Methadone may be more addictive and result in more severe withdrawal symptoms than heroin (Burr, 1987).

Conclusions

Research on different treatments does give some evidence that crime and other harms are reduced for those undergoing treatment. These evaluations, however, are generally based on those who have sought such treatment. Answers to questions about the benefits of expanding a service to new client groups, through diversion schemes for example, can only be based on the benefits experienced by current client groups, which are known to be older, more likely to be male, less likely to be from ethnic minorities, and more likely to be longer-term, more dependent users of opiates. Effectiveness is likely to vary with treatment population characteristics such as age and other unknown factors (Burr, 1987).

Given the complexity of the drugs-crime relationship, there is no clear reason to believe that reductions in drug use or expenditure on drug use will in themselves result in commensurate reductions in crime, especially when there are no changes in individuals' circumstances (Burr, 1987; Whynes, 1991). There is sufficient evidence, however, to be able to conclude that there is an association between individuals voluntarily undergoing treatment programmes, and a reduction in the level of their criminal activity. This may partly be because voluntary referral reflects other important changes in the individual's circumstances. It must be borne in mind when developing indicators that changes in behaviour will be gradual and attempts to detoxify and discharge patients rapidly will be counter-productive (Senay, 1985).

5. Enforcement strategies

The effectiveness of enforcement strategies in affecting drug dealing and drug use is likely to depend on the perceived probability of arrest and expected punishment. It is therefore essential to understand the interactions between the police and the rest of the criminal justice sector (CJS) when developing objective indicators of enforcement strategies.

Drug use and the criminal justice system

A single entry point into the criminal justice system is identifiable: namely arrest by either the police or HM Customs and Excise (see Figure 3). If an individual is arrested there are five possible procedures. If the arrestee is a juvenile, then it may be recommended that they receive a caution at a later date. Alternatively, bail may be given pending further enquiries and/or forensic examination; the charge may be refused, a caution may be given directly; or a charge could be brought. In the case of a charge being brought, the individual will be remanded on bail or held in custody. At this point, the case will be passed to the Crown Prosecution Service. We have concentrated upon the part of this process which is the responsibility of the police. Empirical examination of the work of HM Customs and Excise or other enforcement agencies, and the 'downstream' effects of this process after a suspect is charged (sentencing, recommendations for treatment, or referral by the courts to other agencies in the criminal justice or health systems), is beyond the scope of this project.

Divisional arrests

To enable the research to identify material which could inform the discussion of drugs enforcement output measures at the divisional level, specimen data were collected on drugs arrests on three divisions and interviews were carried out with plain clothes officers. The divisions selected were 'B' (Collyhurst and Grey Mare Lane) 'C' (Longsight and Greenheys/Moss Side) and 'M' (Stretford and Altrincham). These divisions were selected because they appeared to have had a comparable number of drug arrests in the immediately preceding years.

Measurement of divisional arrest output

Data on arrests on the three divisions was collected for two periods: January to March 1993 and January and February 1994, periods separated by the introduction of the new drugs policy on 1 November 1993. These periods were chosen to allow some 'before and after' comparison to be made of similar periods which would be independent of seasonal variation. If six months either side of the implementation date had been chosen, the periods may have not been comparable. In the event, the post-implementation period was limited to two months because it was necessary to finalise the data gathering during March 1994, to enable the analysis to be

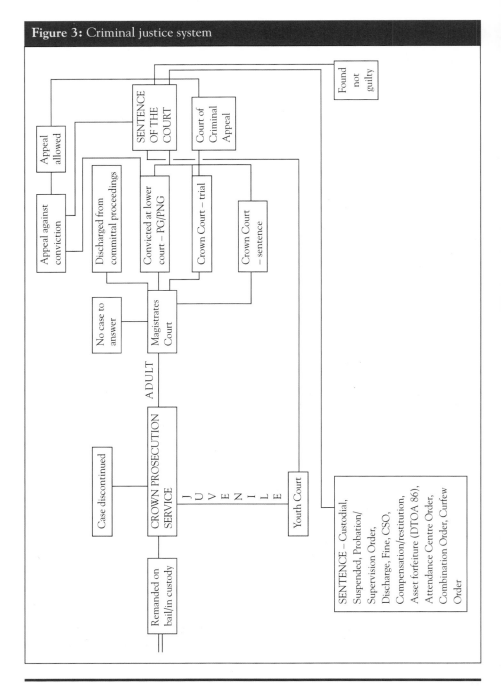

Figure 3: Criminal justice system

completed within the agreed research timetable. It was not thought desirable to include December 1993 arrests to make up a three-month period, in case there was anything distinctively different about the Christmas period.

The data collection instrument focused upon the type of offence charged, the category of drug, charges and cautions, and other measures which have plausibility as indicators of change associated with local police anti-drug strategies. For the analysis, offences involving simple possession, cultivation of small numbers of cannabis plants and permitting premises to be used for smoking cannabis were regarded as 'user-related'. Offences involving supply, possession with intent to supply, production of drugs and conspiracy were regarded as 'trafficking-related'. Similarly, drugs types were aggregated into Class A, Class B (cannabis variants) and Class B plus (amphetamine variants). The last category was distinguished in order to allow cannabis to be analysed separately. The disposal of each case was also documented, being categorised as caution, charge or refused charge. The number of individuals falling into more than one of these categories was in single figures, and thus could be safely discounted for numerical analysis (however interesting such cases might be individually). Case disposal, drug type and offence type (use or trafficking) were analysed against each of the sample periods (1993 contrasted with 1994), for the locations where the offender was charged (contrasting each of the divisions) and against the function of arresting officers (contrasting divisional uniformed and plain clothes officers). This last variable is important for any identification of a shift of focus by plain clothes units (relative to other officers) to so-called 'major dealers' within their locality as required by the strategy.

Units of analysis and performance indicators

A distinction was drawn in collecting the data between an arrest and an arrest-event. The former relates to the arrest of an individual, while the arrest-event may involve a number of arrestees. Arrest-events will yield an identical count to arrestees so long as there is only one arrestee per event. Events which involve more than one arrestee will yield lower counts than of arrests. Events were identified in the course of the data collection but it is upon individual arrests that the following analysis is based. There are advantages and disadvantages in using either event or individual as the primary unit of analysis. Clearly, analysis based upon individual arrests can lead to a degree of double-counting (Chatterton and Frenz, 1993). On the other hand, analysis at the event level understates the numerical importance of multiple arrestees. Currently, police information upon which performance indicators might be based concentrates upon individuals rather than events.

In any final decision about performance indicators it will be necessary to weigh in the balance the merits of the alternative levels of analysis, particularly recognising that the choice of either level will be liable to manipulation. For instance, concentrating on arrest events in performance measurement may encourage officers to arrest people separately who could have been arrested together. Concentrating upon individuals will lead to overestimation of drug quantities by double-counting, unless a more sophisticated measurement system is developed in which elements of both counting units are incorporated. In this section, the unit of analysis is the individual arrest, not the arrest-event.

Missing data and measurement sensitivity

It is important to emphasise that the research was not attempting to identify whether or not there were real increases or decreases in outputs which would underpin quantitative evaluation of the strategy. The exercise was intended to contribute to the development of viable indicators for divisional drugs policing by seeing which variables existed with reasonable uniformity, and whether they appeared sensitive to the kinds of change introduced by the new policy. The difficulties revealed by the 'gaps' in some of the data will be discussed below in the final section of the report. In the case of the divisional data, the identification of a large amount of missing data (particularly in that nearly one-third of the information on the function of arresting officers was missing from the documentation), would have a distorting effect upon measurement (and thereby upon any performance indicator derived from it) which cannot be ignored. Therefore the following should be read in the sense that it is a 'demonstration analysis' for discussion, not as a full evaluation of divisional work on the strategy for the very limited periods which were available for comparison within the scope of this research project. Nonetheless, the data do show which variables moved over the time period and how, and which indices appear insensitive to change (assuming changes really occurred).

Results

When we analysed each of the variables against the 1993 and 1994 samples, the analysis showed that there was no major change in the type of drug or type of offence involved in arrests between the 1993 and 1994 samples. However, there was a shift in who made the arrests; the circumstances in which they were made; how those arrested were processed; a major increase in the rate of cautioning; a slight increase in the number of charges; and a commensurate decrease in the number of refused charges. There was evidence of consistent differences between divisions in charging and cautioning levels.

In the analysis of the total arrests for these divisions, taken as a whole, we found that there was a slight decrease in the number of arrests per month between 1993 and 1994. For example, although the January 1994 arrests (113) were slightly up on January 1993 (108), the February 1994 arrests (102), showed a decrease from those in February 1993 (137).

Arrests for user-related offences decreased slightly from 88% of all drugs arrests effected by divisional officers in 1993 to 84% in 1994, with a corresponding increase in trafficking-related offences from 13% to 16%. These changes were not statistically reliable. There was an increase in drugs arrests effected by divisional uniformed officers and a corresponding decrease in the number of arrests effected by plain clothes officers. The change over time by officer-function was statistically reliable. Arrests by divisional uniformed officers rose from 22% of all arrests to 60%, whereas arrests by plain clothes officers fell from 21% to 14%. Arrests by officers from other divisions and units also fell from 57% to 24%.

There was also a significant difference in arrest totals between year and the division where the offender was detained. Cases in 'B' division rose from 24% of all arrests in these divisions to 33%. On 'C' division they fell very slightly from 50% to 48%. On 'M' division the change was more marked, with a fall from 26% to 19% of all drugs cases on these divisions.

Overall, although the distribution of arrests by offence committed did not change over time, the distribution of arrests by division and by officer-function both changed. This may indicate some change in the targeting of police resources, possibly with uniformed officers working more on street operations and drugs and plain clothes officers working on a smaller number of higher quality targets. Such a change in strategy could account for the apparent reduction in productivity (if measured on arrest figures only) in the plain clothes units.

For 46.7% (282/604) of the total divisional arrests, the type of drug involved was not specified. When all the arrests were analysed against drugs types seized, cases involving Class A drugs increased from 13% to 18% of all drugs seizures: case involving Class B from 31% to 33%: and amphetamines (Class B-plus) from 6% to 11%. Only the last increase was statistically significant. When the frequencies were examined to establish the probable reason for this shift, it was found that it could not be accounted for by any decrease in the number of cases where information about the drug-type was missing from the records between 1993 and 1994. The proportion of these remained fairly constant, with a maximum difference of 0.4% between the years on any drug type. Further analysis of the data showed that the increase of seizures in each drug type could be accounted for by an increased number of cases involving a mix of drug types, although it was impossible to identify a pattern.

The slight increase in the proportion of cases involving Class A drugs and in the proportion of trafficking offences may show that the strategy was being achieved in relation to additional targeting at local level. An increase in the proportion of cannabis variants may be connected to the activity of divisional uniformed officers, possibly indicating increased street policing activity. A significant increase in cases involving amphetamines was also revealed. This is more difficult to explain and may be connected either to availability or to increased police activity against powdered drugs. At a global level this analysis may reflect a shift in targeting of police resources, with (possibly) more uniformed officers working on street operations, and plain clothes and drugs officers working on a smaller number of higher quality targets.

Examination of whether drugs offenders were charged or cautioned showed that there was an increase in the levels of both. Cautions rose from 31% of drugs cases on these divisions in the 1993 sample to 44% in 1994. This was a significant increase. Charges for drugs offences also increased significantly from 30% in 1993 to 38% in 1994. This could be accounted for by a significant decrease in refused charges, from 35% of all drugs detentions to 16%, possibly indicating that a change in stop and search procedures was producing more positive results.

Types of arrest circumstance were analysed by year, to identify whether there was any shift in operational methods which could explain the primary effects discussed above. A significant increase was identified in the number of arrests which resulted from stops in the street for drugs offences. These rose from 24% to 37% of all drugs arrests, tending to confirm the point made above in relation to increased charges and possibly accounted for by higher visibility street policing. There was a significant decrease however, in cases where the suspect had been taken to a police station for search. These fell from 40% of the cases on the three divisions to 19%. These findings may also indicate a change in attitudes or local policies on street searches for drugs. No significant difference was found in relation to the arrests from the execution of search warrants but there was an interesting and significant rise in the number of cases where the observation of dealing led to the arrest. These rose from 2% of all cases on these divisions to 7%, a finding which, if the data were reliable, could have indicated an increase in focus upon trafficking-related offences at the local level.

Conclusions

The divisional arrest indicators which we chose for the survey seemed robust enough to establish some basic facts about the pattern of drugs enforcement on the divisions concerned. They include:

- numbers of arrests;
- offence for which arrested (trafficking or possession);
- class of drugs seized (Class A, B and B-plus); and
- output (charge, refused charge or caution).

These need to be analysed against the independent variables such as location of the arrest (division or unit) and role of arresting officer (uniformed or plain clothes).

Analysis of the arrest circumstances and qualitative data about their work also provides a useful degree of contextualisation and should be included. The indicators need to be standardised (per officer in each division or unit) to provide a meaningful comparison. A considerable amount of further work remains to be done to establish the operational viability of these indicators, including taking into account other factors affecting supply and possession offences, and the eventual disposal of cases within the criminal justice systems or through treatment.

Force drugs squad

The Force drugs squad is headed by a Superintendent and a Chief Inspector who are also responsible for advising the force on drugs issues generally. It comprises of two teams, each commanded by an Inspector. One team includes specialist roles for inspection of pharmacies and for enquiries relating to the precursor chemicals. For operational purposes the teams are not deployed according to territorial responsibility and there is considerable flexibility in their deployment.

At the time of the fieldwork, the squad consisted of 8 sergeants and 19 constables, plus the four management posts. In 1988/89 the squad had contained an additional 9 constables (Wright et al, 1993). 16 of the constables and sergeants (59%) had been in the police service for between 11 and 15 years and only one officer had less than 10 years experience. 30% of officers had been in post less than 10 months, 34% for 12 – 24 months and 36% for between 25 and 83 months, indicating a reasonable balance between experienced and new officers. Only four officers had served for longer than three years and two of these were specialists (chemist inspectors).

The force drugs strategy sets out the main objectives of the drugs squad, which are targeting the activities of major dealers and recovering Class 'A' drugs. Other objectives (which are themselves means towards the achievement of the main objectives) include liaison and promoting joint operations with other enforcement and intelligence agencies; liaison and joint operations with divisional plain clothes units, divisional drugs units and sub-divisions generally; production of a flow of suspect intelligence to the force drugs squad; the regulation of pharmaceutical outlets by chemist inspectors from the drugs squad; developing the use of the Financial Investigation Unit (FIU) by the drugs squad and divisional plain clothes units; developing intelligence based systems and operations; cost-effective use of registered informants; and involvement in drugs prevention initiatives and training.

Drugs squad process assessment – drugs squad officers perceptions on how well the strategy is working

To provide information on the processes and context within which any future performance indicators would operate, a survey of drugs squad officers was carried out. The questions covered attitudes to the force strategy; types of drugs on which officers thought it was appropriate to work; targeting systems; their own criteria for judging unit success; intelligence; liaison and the use of informants.

Squad members proved to have a good level of knowledge of their own drugs squad strategy. They all claimed to have read it and most agreed that it was an appropriate response to the drugs problem in Greater Manchester. Some reservations related to resources and management issues, eg. levels of staffing and finance and the liaison between squad members and management. Internal liaison was mentioned on numerous occasions and the point was made that this needed to be a two-way, not just a top-down process. Some of the undesirable consequences of the strategy were also mentioned. It was argued that the information and intelligence flow would be adversely affected now the strategy dictated that the drugs squad could no longer concern themselves with street level dealers. On arrest these dealers had been a vital source of information about higher level traffickers in the past. 33% of respondents described a variety of other problems, including access to, and incompatibilities between, information technology systems, insufficient training for drugs work and uncertainties about whether pharmaceutical drugs still fell within their remit.

Officers also appeared to be knowledgable about the force drugs strategy and most were in broad agreement that it was an appropriate response. However, 56% had reservations about the policy on cautioning and particularly on the cautioning of individuals found in possession of Class A drugs. It was claimed that this had resulted in the same people being repeatedly cautioned for the same type of offence. A sizeable minority of officers (26%) were critical of the new referral scheme. They questioned whether drug users would be genuinely interested in contacting the agencies lists on the referral cards. A large majority of respondents (69%) said that their work had changed as a result of the implementation of the force drugs strategy. Specific reference was made in this connection to the higher standard of target dealer and to the recent concentration on long-term enquiries.

The drugs squad are expected to liaise with, provide support for, and carry out operations with divisional plain clothes, other forces, the Regional Crime Squad Dedicated Drugs Unit (DDU) and HM Customs and Excise. Drugs squad managers expressed some reservations about this part of the strategy, arguing that their commitment to major dealers limited the amount of assistance they could provide to other units. On the whole they still considered that the level of liaison with these other units was satisfactory.

The drugs squad lower ranks were also dissatisfied with the amount of liaison with the divisional plain clothes and these criticisms were echoed by the divisional plain clothes units. Accusations of elitism were levelled at the drugs squad and examples cited where its members had allegedly failed to use local divisional intelligence and to consult plain clothes staff before carrying out operations. We were advised that a comparison of force drugs squad arrests with those of the plain clothes units would reveal that the quality of their work and the level of their targets was generally no higher. These liaison problems had not been resolved by designating a member of the squad as the liaison officer for a particular division. In the main, good liaison tended to be based on personal contacts established between members of the drugs squad and the plain clothes units at an earlier stage in their service.

This was mentioned several times in connection with the 'C' division where, it is interesting to note, 63% of drugs squad officers had worked with the plain clothes department within the last 12 months. The proportion who reported collaborative work on other divisions was much smaller. The impression gained from most of our interviews with plain clothes unit personnel was that their relationship with the drugs squad was generally poor. Considering the necessary degree of collaboration, this finding is worthy of further investigation. On a cautionary note it is necessary to emphasise that these findings are based on a small number of interviews which may be unrepresentative. The fact that it was not possible to follow up points of criticism should also be borne in mind. These caveats aside, there appears to be sufficient information to suggest that this is a tension area worthy of further investigation.

Nearly three-quarters of lower ranks in the squad thought the relationship between themselves and the DDU needed to be developed. Many considered that more regular meetings might help but only if the fundamental issues of trust and openness were addressed. However the management of the drugs squad and that of the DDU reported there was frequent liaison between themselves and the force drugs squad commanders.

The secondment of officers from H.M. Customs and Excise to the drugs squad was cited as an example of how close the relationship was and we were told of several recent joint operations. Twenty of the squad had worked at different levels of collaboration with H.M. Customs and Excise at international/national level during the previous twelve months.

In summary, these findings indicate that drugs squad officers had reservations about the extent to which the strategy was working in relation to liaison, and to the degree to which they had been able to settle into a system which encouraged them to work on better quality targets. These factors are important intervening variables and will affect the extent to which output performance is seen as realistically achievable by the practitioners.

Prioritising targets

Prioritising work through the adoption of a targeted approach and the choice of targets appropriate to each unit's level of operation is emphasised by both the force and the drugs squad strategies. However, the vagueness of the terminology employed when they described appropriate targets and levels of operation is one of the major problems encountered in evaluating whether units are performing effectively. This will come as no surprise to anyone acquainted with recent drugs literature (Dorn et al, 1992). Throughout both strategy documents repeated reference is made to dealer types and various levels of dealer operations but these are nowhere adequately defined. In the absence of such definitional clarity and specification of the criteria employed, it is difficult for an evaluator to make an independent classification of operations and of arrests made by a particular unit, with the aim of assessing how many fall within their appropriate target category.

The drugs squad's classification system aims to promote more effective use of resources by specifying the types of activity which can be performed on the different categories of targets. It describes the activities in the following ways:

Category 'A': These operations involve the use of covert surveillance, participating informants, undercover operations or technical facilities. They are authorised at Detective Superintendent level. They require an operational name allocated by the force criminal intelligence office and necessitate flagging by the National Criminal Intelligence Service (NCIS). Some Category 'A' targets will have been Category 'B' and Category 'C' targets and will have been through a process of negotiation with management to establish them as Category 'A'. The drugs squad can run two Category 'A' targets at any one time with all officers being used to their maximum.

Category 'B': Each officer of the drugs squad is encouraged to nominate a long-term target. This entails the gathering of information and intelligence with a view to taking action under other categories if it become appropriate. Such targets are approved by the Detective Inspectors and reviewed on a two-month basis. An operational name is also obtained from the force criminal intelligence office and flagging or interest markers are placed in NCIS.

Category 'C': Targets under this category are those which require short term surveillance or observation and are authorised by Detective Sergeants. An operational name is not obtained for these cases but the target's name is logged with the drugs squad intelligence officer.

Category 'D': This involves the obtaining of a search warrant following the receipt and verification of information. No separate authorisation is necessary but the target name is logged with the drugs squad intelligence officer.

Category 'X': Targets in this category are those which are passed to divisions or which are considered to be pending. Any decision to take no further action or to regard a target in this category as pending must be taken by at least the Detective Chief Inspector (Force Drugs Squad Operations, 1993).

No explanation is provided in this document of the criteria used by drugs squad members and their managers when they are using this classification system and negotiating into which category a particular target fits. The document produces an additional area of confusion as far as the evaluation of drugs squad work is concerned. It appears to suggest that members of the squad may legitimately perform work on individuals who are not major dealers ie. categories 'C', 'D' and 'X'.

We explored this issue in the interviews. Officers were first asked to use the drugs squad target categories and the four Broome Report categories of major international dealer, major dealer (force area), street level drugs dealers, and user, to classify their last five arrests. Having established how many lower level arrests they had made and, in the process of doing that, whether they were able to equate the Broome categories with the squad target categories, we then asked them to classify the people they were currently working on into the latter categories. 78 arrests were examined and 33 of these appear to have been at the 'appropriate' target level, falling into the drugs squad target categories 'A' or 'B' and into the Broome Report category for major dealers. 30 arrests, classified as 'C', 'D' or 'X' cases, were placed into the Broome categories for street dealer or user. This suggests that some officers equate 'C', 'D' and 'X' categories with street dealers. By extension it might be inferred that the squad target categorisation system permits them to concentrate on these users and dealers. The officers were then asked to classify the targets they were currently working on, using the drugs squad target category. Targets at the Broome user and street dealer level were being worked on by almost half of the officers and most members of the squad said they were working on so many category 'D' and 'X' targets that they could not enumerate them. They explained that many of the 'X' targets would be passed on to divisional plain clothes in due course.

Additional interview data provide a further indication that the squad members were targeting their work on categories which the force strategy would describe as being beneath their level of operation. Nearly two thirds (63)% were working on suspects who were not classified targets. One explanation for this may be that the interpretations they placed on the official categories were different from those we inferred. If this is the case it reinforces the earlier point about the requirement for clear definitions. Another explanation may be that the drugs squad not infrequently work on targets that initially appeared to be potential category 'A' or 'B' targets but which subsequent enquiries revealed to be minor ones. To an extent that we have been unable to document in this study, they may have to follow-up on information reportedly on a 'major dealer' only to find that it relates to a user or street level dealer. Unless some other unit is given responsibility for these initial enquiries and screens out 'inappropriate cases' for the drugs squad, it is difficult to see how they could avoid working on and investigating some lower level targets, in the process of building up their category 'A' and 'B' cases. The implications of these findings for targeting and evaluation will be discussed below after we have examined additional data on the arrests made by members of the squad.

Seizure data and drugs squad arrests

According to the drugs squad arrest book, its members made 111 arrests between 1 January 1993 and 10 May 1994. These arrests related to 95 arrest-events indicating that in several cases a number of people had been arrested in connection with the same incident. 65 arrests occurred prior to the introduction of the strategy (1 March 1993 to 31 October 1993) and 33 arrests in the post-implementation period (1 November 1993 to 10 May 1994). In 7 other cases, the person arrested was not charged with a drugs offence but with offences of handling, theft, etc. In another 5 cases, details about the arrest were not available and in 1 case there was no charge.

Type of drug

Although the strategies of both the drugs squad and the force specify Class 'A' drugs as the target of drugs squad work, a relatively large proportion of arrests in both time periods involved Class 'B' drugs. Table 11 shows that in the pre-implementation period there were 18 (28%) arrests involving Class 'A' drugs, 38 (58%) arrests involving Class 'B' cannabis-variant drugs and 15 (23%) arrests involving class 'B-plus' amphetamine-variant drugs. In the later period there were 14 (42%) arrests connected with Class 'A' drugs , 13 (39%) arrests involving Class 'B' cannabis-variant drugs and 9 (27%) arrests involving Class 'B-plus' amphetamine-variant drugs. Had there been a greater number of cases involving a combination of Class A and Class B drugs this might have helped to explain why so many Class 'B' cases were found among the drugs squad arrests. In fact, there were only 2 cases in 1993 and 4 cases in 1994 where Class A and B drugs were combined (see tables 12 and 13), although the overlap between Class B and Class B-plus was much greater.

Class of drug	Pre-implementation period		Post-implementation period	
	%	(n)	%	(n)
Class 'A'	28	(18)	42	(14)
Class 'B' (Cannabis variants)	58	(38)	39	(13)
Class 'B-plus' (Amphetamine variants)	23	(15)	27	(9)

Table 11: Drugs squad arrests shown by class of drug involved and period when arrest occured

Tables 12 and 13 describe in more detail the arrests made by the squad before (table 12) and after (table 13) the introduction of the force drugs strategy. In the arrest period before the introduction of the Force strategy (01.01.93 – 31.10.93), 42% (27/65) of the arrests related to cannabis (resin and/or herbal) offences alone; in the later period (01.11.93 -10.05.94), the proportion of these arrests decreased to 21% (7/33). In the earlier arrest period, 23% (15/65) of arrests involved heroin; in the later period these arrests increased to 30% (10/65). In 33% (5/15) and 60% (6/10) of these cases respectively heroin was seized in combination with another type of Category A drug, usually crack. Only one arrest for cocaine was made and this appeared in the earlier period.

Table 12: Drugs squad arrests and type and amount of drugs seized (01.01.93 – 31.10.93

Case No	Type and amount of drugs seized (grams)						
	Herbal	Resin	Amphet	Cocaine	Crack	Heroin	Other
1			28.0g				
2		42kg					
3		42kg					
4		42kg					
5		392.0	28.0				30 LSD+ mushrms.
6	2000.0						
7						14.0	
8			1000.0				
9		5.0	2000.0				
10		5.0	2000.0				
11		40.0	3.0				
12						6.0	
13	*						Over 100 cannibis plants
14					200.0	25.0	
15		26.4					
16						0.7	
17						0.7	
18					11.5		
19							Supplier no drugs recovered 334 ml. Methadne
20						5.0	
21	250.0	500.0					
22		28.0	28.0				
23					10.0	8.0	
24		56.0					
25					0.2	3.2	
26			120.0				
27						15.0	
28		500.0	500.0				
29			500.0				
30						505.0	
31				82.0		505.0	
32						505.0	
33			160 Tabs				
34	3.0	2.0					
35					0.2		
36	28.0						
37		1.0					
38		28.0					
39		10.0					

Case No	Type and amount of drugs seized (grams)						
	Herbal	Resin	Amphet	Cocaine	Crack	Heroin	Other
40		2.0					
41						0.2	
42		28.0					
43							4 LSD
44		1.0					
45		2.0					
46			14.0				
47			*				
48		28.0					
49							1 box of Temgesic
50	1.0						
51		5.0					
52							1 ecstsy
53		2.0	3.0				1 cannabis plant
54	1.0						
55		2.0					
56		5.0				0.1	
57		28.0					
58		3.0					
59		30.0					
60		*					
61		2.0					
62			5.0				
63		30.0					
64		5.0	20.0				
65						0.2	

In tables 12 and 13 the following should be noted:

* indicates seizure of a quantity of a drug of this type where the weight was not shown on the returned questionnaire

Case No	Type and amount of drugs seized (grams)						
	Herbal	Resin	Amphet	Cocaine	Crack	Heroin	Other
1			20.0				
2					10.0		
3					1.7	2.7	
4	203.0	295.0	347.0		662.0	1691.0	27ml methadne + ecstasy
5			8.9				
6		10.0					
7		*	*			*	
8			30.0				
9					80.0	90.0	
10					80.0	90.0	
11			10.0		80.0	90.0	
12					80.0	90.0	
13		30.0				1.0	
14					56.0		
15							Supply ecstasy no drugs recovered
16			982.0				
17						0.1	
18	9.8						Undated
19		7.0	5.0				
20		*					500 gms paracetamol
21	10.0						
22	1.0						
23		*					
24	*						
25		3.0					
26	1.0		1.0				
27						3.2	
28							none recovered
29							
30		10.0					
31			30.0				
32							334 ml methadne
33							Quantity Temazpm.

Table 13: Drugs squad arrests and type and amount of drugs seized (01.11.93 – 10.05.94)

In tables 12 and 13 the following should be noted:

* indicates seizure of a quantity of a drug of this type where the weight was not shown on the returned questionnaire

Quantity of drugs

The variation in the quantities of drugs seized is considerable. There was an exceptionally large seizure of 1691 grammes of heroin in the later period and 505 grammes in the earlier period. The proportion of cases where small quantities of heroin, less than 1 gramme and less than 6 grammes, were seized was also high in both years. A wide range of seizures is also noticeable in the case of cannabis where the small quantities seized are perhaps more remarkable given the fact that this is a Class B and therefore not a 'target' drug.

Arrest circumstances

In both periods, over two thirds (69%) of those arrested were subsequently charged and with the exception of one person, the remainder were cautioned. In 46 (47%) of arrests the arrestee was charged with possession, in 19 (19%) with dealing and in 33 (34%) with both possession and dealing.

Each member of the drug squad was asked to complete a form for each arrest giving details of the circumstances of the arrest. The information provided on these self-completion arrest forms was disappointing. In the largest proportion of cases (67%), the offenders were simply said to have been arrested following the execution of a search warrant. No details were provided about the enquiries and information which led to the taking out of the warrant. The original intention had been to use the details of the circumstances leading up to the arrests to classify them as contingent, tactical or strategic. Contingent arrests are those which happened fortuitously, rather than as a planned outcome; tactical arrests are those which happen as the result of planned operation but not necessarily because of the strategy; strategic arrests are those which resulted from activity which was directly encouraged by the force strategy. The arrests shown below provide examples of both contingent and tactical arrests. For example, case 7, which relates to an arrest after a targeted surveillance, was tactical. Case 6, which related to an arrest for a large quantity of cannabis (42 kg) consequent upon the arrest of a man for stealing a car from a hotel car park, could be said to be fortuitous or contingent. Neither of these arrests could strictly be said to have been carried out directly as a result of following the force strategy.

Case 1

Acting upon information "from a reliable source" that a large quantity of drugs were in the possession of the arrested person at his home address, a search warrant was executed. A small amount of cannabis was found and the person arrested.

Case 2

Officers of the drug squad maintained surveillance on the suspect who was seen to deal to a number of people on the street. 3 grammes of herbal cannabis and 2 grammes of resin were seized when he was arrested for a trafficking and using offence.

Case 3

Following a complaint from a parent that her daughter was being supplied with cannabis by a colleague at work, the suspect's premises were searched by the divisional plain clothes unit and a small quantity of cannabis was recovered.

Case 4

Following a complaint from neighbours that a particular dwelling was being used for dealing purposes, a search warrant was executed at the premises by the divisional plain clothes unit and a small amount of cannabis was seized.

Case 5

Drugs squad officers entered a betting office and searched a person suspected of abusing controlled drugs. He was arrested and subsequently cautioned for possession of under a gramme of cannabis resin. In this case the person's arrest was connected with his status as an informant.

Case 6

A man arrested after stealing a car from a hotel car park. The vehicle contained 42 kilogrammes of cannabis resin. The man told the officers where he had stolen the vehicle and drugs squad officers went to the hotel and arrested two other men. All three men was charged with possession and possession within intent to supply.

Case 7

This arrest was the result of a targeted operation carried out in conjunction with another force. After long-term observation and surveillance the arrested person was seen to supply cocaine. He was followed to commercial premises in Manchester. A search warrant was executed and the man was arrested in possession of a half-kilogram of heroin. Two other people were also arrested. The first man was charged with supplying cocaine and all three were jointly charged with possessing the heroin.

It has not been possible, because of these difficulties, to classify the arrests into the categories we had originally intended. However the use of street stops which produced 11% of the arrests, and observations of dealing which produced a further 9% would appear on surface inspection to be higher than would be expected for a squad focusing on major dealers. By the same token the proportion of arrests resulting from targeted operations is surprisingly small.

Trafficking and user cases

Both the drugs squad and the force strategies targeted the drugs squad on high level dealers. It seems reasonable, therefore, to expect that a large proportion of the persons arrested would have been charged with offences of trafficking rather than possession. In practice it was difficult to classify arrests into these two categories because a large proportion of arrested persons were charged with both types of offence as alternatives (see table 14).

Table 14: Offences with which arrested persons were charged shown by period in which arrests occured

	Pre-implementation period		Post-implementation period	
	%	(n)	%	(n)
Trafficking offences	18	(12)	21	(7)
Possession offences	48	(31)	45	(15)
Both	34	(22)	33	(11)

Conclusion

Precise target categories and a clearly understood classification system are prerequisites for both effective targeting and evaluation purposes. The confusion revealed in the interviews with drugs squad members regarding target definitions and their selection of lower-level, seemingly inappropriate, targets will need to be addressed if management wish their officers to be more focused in their work. Unless targets and objectives are explicitly identified, prior to work being carried out on them, when it comes to performance evaluation it is impossible to determine whether members of the unit have been correctly focused and hence to assess their outputs. In later sections of the report we shall provide further evidence that the use of performance indicators and the assessment of results needs to be carried out in the context of the objectives of the unit in question.

According to the seizure data and the information about the charges it is clear that the drugs squad failed to make the kinds of arrests the force strategy demanded of them. However, before any conclusions about effectiveness are drawn from the information provided by these indicators, more needs to be learnt about the squad's work and any systems and processes that it relied upon to achieve its goals. Without these additional data the meaning of the information provided by the seizure and charge indicators and their policy implications, are unclear. These issues are addressed below.

6. Conclusions

Performance indicators and evaluation

This research has used a range of data-collection instruments, providing indicators for a preliminary evaluation of the GMP strategy. In some cases the data related directly to potential output indicators which were our primary focus. In other cases, data were collected to provide contextual information on intervening variables. The surveys were also a means of testing the viability of collecting such data.

In each of the above sections, the findings on aspects of the enforcement and diversionary elements of the strategy have been discussed. Some aspects of the relationship between drugs and crime (see section 3) have been explored and further monitoring of the drugs-crime connection suggested, using the drugs-involvement indicators developed here. These include previous drugs convictions; finding drugs or drugs-related items on the arrested person or in their home or work premises; whether they requested medication; and whether they made any admission that the offence for which they had been arrested had been committed to finance a drugs habit.

On enforcement, the indicators used in the divisional arrest survey (see section 5) included numbers of arrests; the offence for which arrested; class of drugs seized; and whether the person was charged, subject to a refused charge or cautioned. For the drugs squad and other units concentrating on drugs work, precise target categories related to the objectives are prerequisites for both effective targeting and evaluation. As in the instance of divisional cases, seizure and arrest data are crucial indicators, as are the circumstances of the arrests. All these indicators will need to be analysed against the independent variables such as division or unit and role of arresting officer. They will also need to be standardised (per officer) to provide meaningful comparison.

A considerable amount of further work remains to be done to establish the viability of these indicators before they can be applied to a full operational evaluation. In order to interpret the data provided by output and outcome indicators, and thereby derive some conclusions about effectiveness, attention also needs to be paid to the role of intervening factors. We have argued that the impact made by any strategy and tactic is influenced by additional variables which may facilitate or detract from performance. To interpret the results of strategic and tactical initiatives, therefore, the mediating effect of these factors must be considered. Otherwise poor outcomes will be attributed to faults which are perceived to be inherent in the strategies or tactics themselves. This could lead to a strategy being abandoned when its potential for success, given the right conditions, is very high. We shall discuss this with reference to our findings in the area of enforcement and particularly the work of the drugs squad.

Interpreting the meaning of performance indicators

The analysis of drugs squad arrests, using seizure data i.e. types and amounts of drugs seized, and the offences charged, revealed that the squad generally failed to achieve its objective of targeting on high level dealers who were trafficking in Class 'A' drugs. This is valuable information but as it stands it is not sufficient for evaluation purposes. Management are entitled to ask why the goals set for the drugs squad by the strategy were not achieved and what can be done to improve their performance. The attempt to answer those questions demands a more comprehensive analysis and that analysis, we shall suggest, requires the development of additional indicators. Those indicators would not examine the outputs or outcomes of the activities of squad members. They would be situated to collect information about systems and processes on which the effectiveness of their performance is contingent. Rigorous evaluation, in other words, requires an explanation of the meaning of data provided by output and outcome indicators and that in turn necessitates an examination of the quality of inputs and other intervening factors. Without this information no conclusions can be derived about effectiveness and how it might be improved.

Intervening variables

It was argued earlier that the effective performance of any unit in relation to its objectives, is contingent upon the operation of a number of exogenous and

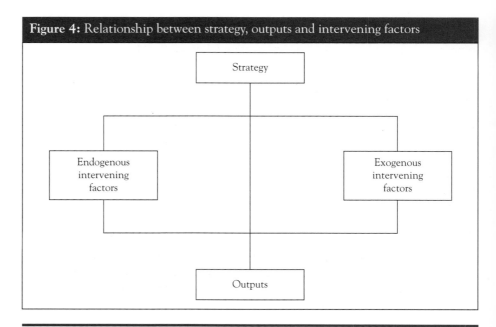

Figure 4: Relationship between strategy, outputs and intervening factors

endogenous intervening factors. Figure 4 illustrates the point. It would be possible to extend this model to include other dimensions of the strategy and to incorporate outcomes and the factors that intrude between outputs and outcomes. Because of the limitations of space the discussion will focus on the enforcement aspects of the strategy and outputs in that area.

The endogenous factors are potentially more amenable to control than exogenous factors because they are internal to the organisation. The influence of the latter originates in the organisation's often chaotic and unpredictable environment and they introduce a large element of uncertainty into the work situation. When drugs enforcement officers described themselves as being "zapped by exocet missiles" which unexpectedly came at them "from out of the blue", they were referring to the intrusion of these unpredictable, external factors which disrupted their plans and sometimes ruined their operations. However, although the operation of exogenous factors can have a devastating effect on what is achieved, skilfully managed and adequately resourced internal support systems can sometimes reduce their impact, even if it cannot totally eliminate them.

The key questions are whether the police can exercise any control over the intervening variables which will otherwise determine how successful they are, and if they can, whether they are exercising that control in practice. This leads into an investigation of organisational systems that have been developed for managing information, planning operations, monitoring the work process etc. Part of the failure to meet performance targets that is attributed to exogenous "exocets" may sometimes be the result of "friendly fire" ie the ineffective performance of internal support systems and processes. Implementation failure, lack of forward planning, poor information systems, low levels of skill reflecting deficiencies in the provision of relevant training, can be hidden if there is an exclusive emphasis on the unpredictable, environmental factors. In conclusion we suggest that, given the importance of these internal systems and processes, as the drivers of the strategy, it would be useful to develop a further set of indicators to monitor their performance. This would enable management to maintain a watchful eye on their effectiveness (and thereby exercise some influence on general output of a unit in relation to its objectives). These indicators would also provide the valuable contextual information that is needed to explain the variations in levels of achieved output over time and between units.

Target categorisation, objective setting systems and performance outputs

The target classification and objective setting systems are important for both focusing and evaluation purposes. The analysis of the drugs squad interview data revealed the deficiencies of their target classification system. A large number of the targets of the officers and the arrests they described, suggest they were focused on objectives that were not directly related to the strategy but we cannot be sure that this was the case. Unless their objectives are known it is difficult to know what to make of information on their outputs. What were they trying to achieve? Did these objectives change over the period under consideration? Were they different from the objectives of other units with which their performance might be compared? Having used performance indicators to obtain output data, in this instance seizures and charges, it is necessary to contextualise those data with reference to the stated objectives of the unit to be assessed. The contrast between the B and C division plain clothes units illustrates this point well.

These units were operating with an identical actual strength of one sergeant and ten constables but at the time of the interviews the function of the two units, and therefore their objectives in relation to drugs, were very different. The 'B' division plain clothes unit performed the conventional, multi-functional role which has been common on the Manchester inner-city divisions for many years. In addition to drugs, the unit was responsible for licensing, prostitution, importuning, malicious telephone calls and letters, making enquiries into absconders, etc. The arrests recorded by one of the constables in his pocket-book confirmed the multifarious nature of the work.

This unit was primarily a reactive drugs unit in the sense that it relied upon complaints from 'ordinary' members of the public as its primary source of information about dealers and drug dealing locations. Once a complaint was received an action sheet would be issued to a member of the unit to enquire into the allegation. If it was substantiated and the circumstances warranted it, supervision would then authorise further surveillance or organise a raid. Cases 3 and 4 in the arrest cases listed earlier are illustrations of the type of arrest produced by this unit. Infrequent use was made by the unit of cultivated informants. One officer was described to be exceptional in having two registered informants. We would anticipate that persons arrested for drugs offences by this unit would typically be low level dealers selling mainly 'for personal use'.

In contrast, the plain clothes unit on the 'C' division functioned as a specialist divisional drugs squad. Officers interviewed from this unit referred to receiving information from registered informants and the force drugs squad. We would expect the arrest and seizure data for this unit to be consistent with a focus on high level divisional dealers in Class A drugs.

In view of their different types of target and corresponding differences in their objectives it would not be sensible to compare the seizure and charge data of these two units to decide which was the more effective of the two. Each unit's output has to be viewed in the context of their objective(s). In the case of the B division unit this was to respond to annoyance caused to residents by localised drug abuse and drug dealing. In the instance of the C division unit the objective was to target on local high level dealers.

The importance of knowing the stated objectives of a unit as the context against which its performance can be assessed can be further illustrated with reference to the operations of one of the uniformed sections examined in this study. The sub-divisional commander used a number of high profile uniformed policing operations to target street dealers and disrupt their business. A number of arrests were made as a result of these swoops but we were informed that only relatively small quantities of drugs were seized. However, the important point about these operations is that they were aimed at reassuring the people living in those areas that the police locally were manifestly concerned about the drugs problem. Seizure data were not strictly relevant to the assessment of the operations. Their effectiveness was to be judged with reference to the objective of providing public reassurance which might be assessed through a survey of public satisfaction.

Management in the drugs squad were unable easily to provide data on the target classification of the people arrested by its members. Had this information been readily available to us it might have explained why they had made so many seemingly incongruous arrests. An unspecified number of those arrested might have proved to have been Category A or B targets and the arrests may have been the result of a targeted operation but the seizures may still have been poor because of the intervention of a number of unanticipated and unavoided factors. For example, it may have been necessary to observe the person complete several deals before arresting him, the dealer may have been able to react quickly and dispose of most of the drugs before he was arrested etc.

These examples should suffice to illustrate the importance of the systems which produce and record targets and objectives and to emphasize the need to contextualise information from output indicators with reference to those specific targets and objectives. Note should be taken of the problems that would be encountered in any attempt to interpret aggregate data, using standardised performance indicators, which relate to units with different objectives and targets.

The quality of other internal resource systems that intervene between strategy and output

The outputs of units such as the divisional plain clothes and force drugs squad have to be contextualised with reference to the size of their establishment, whether they were specialist drugs units etc . This is not surprising. What proved to be of particular interest when we came to examine the results of this study, was how it had extended our understanding of what constitutes an input and how important the quality of these internal factors is. The issue of resource inputs is not simply a question of *how many* man-hours and items of equipment are deployed on various kinds of drugs enforcement activities. It is a question of *how* they were deployed and targeted, and also of whether officers were trained adequately to perform their roles, whether the support systems designed to assist them were performing that function effectively and so on. As the intervening variables listed in Figure 5 indicate, our investigation of inputs took us into a consideration of internal resource systems. We now see these as 'drivers' of the strategy which exercise a variable influence on the work of drugs enforcement officers.

Several of the systems identified here affect the way that information is obtained, recorded, analysed and distributed to those who need it, ie information-processing and handling systems. The informant registration and handling systems play a key role in the information generation process. It would be of interest to determine whether there are performance indicators which could be used to assess how well these systems are working. How variable is the quality and quantity of information

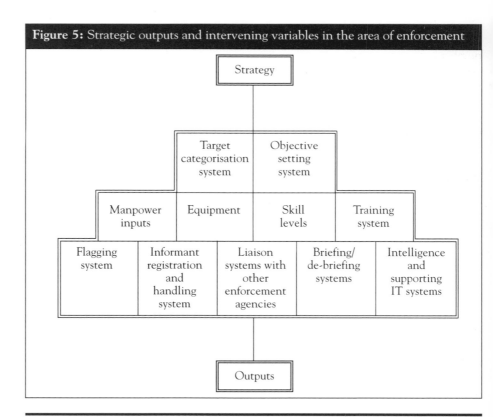

Figure 5: Strategic outputs and intervening variables in the area of enforcement

inputted into these systems by enforcement officers? Can a disproportionate number of failed or aborted operations be attributed to particular informants?

Briefing and de-briefing systems were also shown to be variable in the frequency they were used and in their quality. We noted instances where a team of officers was held on stand-by for a raid for some time and then told that it had been called off. How frequently does this occur and what reasons are given for it? How often are raids carried out and warrants executed with negative results? How effective is the system of de-briefing which enquires into why a raid was cancelled and assesses the information underpinning such operations and its quality?

Interviews with the drugs squad and plain clothes units identified deficiencies in the quality of liaison systems. The quality of the liaison systems and their effectiveness in promoting the flow of information between units involved in drugs enforcement work cannot be ignored in any assessment of the strategy.

These systems are so crucial to the success of the strategy that it would pay the Greater Manchester Police to undertake a review of their effectiveness. Ideally a number of indicators could be developed to monitor their effectiveness. A small number of such measures, strategically placed to key into core processes involved in each system, would enable routine monitoring and provide the information needed to interpret the results from output indicators.

The following improvements that we recommend to information systems for evaluation purposes would also prove relevant to the auditing of these intervening systems.

Information audit

The preliminary work undertaken for this project highlights the need to develop accurate information databases, if objective indicators are to be implemented. Such indicators need to be not only conceptually robust, but also capable of being derived from operational data collected by the police. The first stage in this process, however, is to undertake an information audit, and this is one of the major recommendations of this research project. The audit carried out in Manchester is described further in this section.

The primary sources of documentation which were used in gathering data on drugs arrests were the index to persons detained (Greater Manchester Police forms 804 and 804A), custody records, prosecution files held in the Administration of Justice Units (AJUs), and cautioning forms (Greater Manchester Police form 309). Figure 6 indicates how these data were collected:

Figure 6: Administration of Justice Unit casefiles flowchart

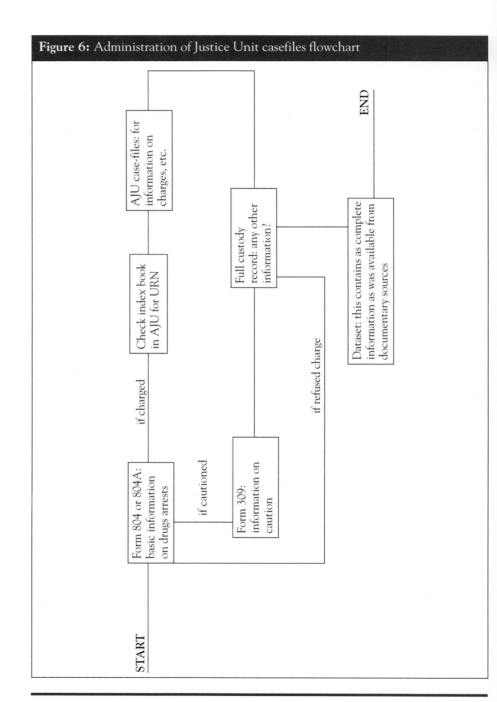

Greater Manchester Police indices of detained persons

The form 804 in 1993 and the 804A (revised edition) in 1994 were used in the first instance to capture basic data on persons detained in connection with drugs offences. The information collected from this source was the date of arrest, name of detained person, address, CRO number, race code, occupation and offence for which detained. The revised form, 804A, recorded this information in a more accessible format for performance measurement purposes, and contained additional information on the duty of the arresting officer which had previously not been available on the 804 necessitating a trawl through other documentary sources. The details provided on these forms were taken by GMP personnel from the information on custody records. The variable accuracy, completeness and presentation of this transferred information proved to be an important factor in the data collection exercise.

On one of the sites, all the 804 forms were missing due to recent office relocation and this entailed the fieldworkers going to the original custody records to identify the drug arrests. On another site, photocopies of the 804 and 804A forms were made available and these proved to be more difficult to read. Due to the way in which these forms were compiled, there were cases where material was not retrievable from this source.

AJU index book/card index

Additional data was obtained from case files kept in sub divisional Administration of Justice Units (AJUs). These files provided information on the charge, circumstances of the arrest, the type and amount of drugs seized and the court outcome. In order to locate every file, the index book containing a list of all prisoners and their file numbers, i.e. the unique reference number (URN), was used. Linking a particular arrest with the URN proved to be a problem because no arrest date was recorded. For example, if someone had been arrested 3 times, they would have 3 URNs and this meant the researcher had to check them all to find the event relevant to the data collection period. This was the same in 4 out of the 6 sites examined. The remaining 2 had card indexes with the date of arrest recorded.

AJU casefiles

These files contained summaries of evidence, statements, exhibits lists, forensic statements and other papers relevant to the court appearance. Although files in the AJUs were generally well-managed, in those instances where the case papers were not ordered in a systematic way, more time had to be spent locating the relevant information. A proposed AJU computer system will solve most of these problems.

There were instances where the files were missing or did not contain the relevant information e.g. unless the drugs had been submitted to the forensic laboratory, information on type and amounts of drugs was often unavailable; detailed information on mode of investigation or arrest was not easy to find if summaries of evidence were missing or witness statements were incomplete.

It should be noted that files for the January – March 1993 period were more accessible than those for the January – February 1994 period because the latter were still in the process of being completed for submission to the Crown Prosecution Service (CPS) or with the CPS. This should be borne in mind when considering collecting this type of data as it will have implications on the completeness of the material.

Custody records

Custody records were inspected primarily for the information on the circumstances relating to refused charges contained on a sheet normally attached to the custody record. In many cases, these sheets were not with the custody records. In these instances only basic data could be collected and information on the circumstances of the arrest etc. was not available. The custody records were also used to fill gaps in data already collected from the other documentary sources e.g. race codes, doctors' attendance etc. They became the final check for missing data. Custody records were generally well kept on the divisions where the fieldwork was undertaken. The process for locating missing custody records would be impossible and far too time consuming to undertake, particulary for custody records from 1993.

Cautioning records (Form 309)

Cautioning records were a key source for gathering additional information about cases where a caution had been given. These forms were attached to the appropriate custody record. However, many of the 309s had not been attached to custody records. At two of the sites, the 309s were dealt with by a dedicated clerk at the Divisional station; this proved to be a more effective way of retaining them.

Quality of the information contained in GMP systems

Details about the custody office and the date of arrest were always recorded on the forms 804 and 804A. It was assumed that this information had been accurately copied from the custody records.

There were 200 cases (33%) where the department of the arresting officer was not available from the index of detained persons form. The form 804 did not have a specific section for recording this, but even on the form 804A, which introduced a section for this purpose, there were instances where this information was not provided. Although a search was made in the other documents, in many cases the branch of the arresting officer was not found. This loss of data seriously restricted the type of analysis that could be made on the arrests.

In 447 cases (74%), the location of the offence was not recorded. In the remaining cases, the information was found on the cautioning record, refused charge sheet or AJU case file.

In 61 cases (10%), it was not possible to identify the circumstances of the arrest using the summaries of evidence, witness statements etc. in the AJU case files, the refused charge sheets or custody records. Even when these circumstances were recorded, they were described in such broad, global terms such as "a search warrant was executed", " as a result of information received", "following a street stop/search" etc. that only a relatively crude categorisation was possible. As a consequence the information on circumstances of arrest provided only basic data such as the number of stop/searches of persons/vehicles in the street, number of search warrants executed, number of stop/detentions for drugs search/interview at the police station, number of arrests in connection with another offence, number of arrests as a result of observed dealing, and number of arrests in connection with a targeted operation. The information did not enable us to make any assessment of whether an arrest was strategic, tactical or contingent.

In almost half of all the arrests the weight of drugs seized was not recorded although references were found to the recovery of "small quantities". For instance, the precise weights seized were provided in only 33% of cocaine arrests, 30% crack cocaine arrests and 25% of heroin arrests. The significance of this missing information will become apparent later in the discussion of how the type and amount of seizures assist in the development of performance indicators.

Other information relevant to the development of these indicators was impossible to find in the documentary sources examined. An attempt was made to determine whether any financial enquiries had been made under the provisions of the Drugs Trafficking Offences Acts, into the finances of the arrested person. This information was provided on only 4 cases.

Collectability of the information

Even though skilled researchers, with a good knowledge of policing systems, were used for the collection of these data, it took 50.5 fieldworker-days to complete the exercise. These costs will obviously need to be borne in mind in the development of performance indicators and the expense involved in providing the information to derive them. Computer-based information systems, such as the proposed force pilot scheme for computerising custody records, should assist in resolving many of these difficulties. It is important that they are designed with performance evaluation requirements in mind and that any data entered are accurate and exhaustive.

Outputs

A good deal of the research effort invested in this project has been directed at developing instruments to capture output-relevant data. The force will obviously want to consider whether it wishes to continue to collect these data. If it does we would recommend a number of refinements to the instruments in the light of our experience. For example in the case of the drugs-crime questionnaire it would be worth exploring how recently the arrested person's last drugs conviction was and, given the fact that this was the most frequently used indicator, whether the information could be obtained from the criminal record office at less cost than a questionnaire to arresting officers. In any further surveys it would also be important to record the employment status of the arrested person. It would be possible to continue to track the future involvement of these arrested persons in crime and in treatment.

The problems in obtaining information for the drugs arrest data form were described above. As an alternative we have suggested that first line supervisors may be able to provide this information, although we suspect that this will apply more to sergeants in drugs and plain clothes units than uniformed supervisors. The importance of configuring the data in order that arrested persons and arrest events can be examined separately should be borne in mind.

The interviews with plain clothes and drugs squad officers would be worth repeating at some point in our opinion. The interviews with agency personnel and addicts suggest that it would be possible to identify in each police sub-division a number of people with varying connections with the drugs market who could be consulted about the effects of enforcement and treatment initiatives.

Downstream effects in the criminal justice system have not been assessed during this project but it is arguably necessary for this to be done later, if unit, divisional and force outputs are to be related to outcomes. Similarly, as we have discussed in relation to the *drugs/crime* relationship and referral scheme, it will be necessary to include suitable comparative indicators which show the extent to which there is an impact on drug related offences.

At the level of outcome indicators, a more holistic assessment of outcome performance against the market will be necessary, making regular use of instruments such as user-surveys and agency surveys of the kind we have demonstrated, although it is likely the indicators generated will be indirect or proxy indicators, rather than absolute indicators of the relationship between the market and police interventions.

In summary therefore, we recommend further work to develop a database and a practical set of indicators from the above material. Given the reservations which have been discussed, a formative pilot study using the indicators in conjunction with the practitioners will be required. We suggest that this should continue in collaboration with GMP but progressively, to include other forces. Although this approach may seem over-cautious, the importance and complexity of the subject makes it imperative to be rigorous and to develop systems which have the ultimate support of practitioners at every level, and of other agencies working in the field.

It was emphasised in section 2 of this report that the measurement of performance is complex and potentially misleading, even on a conceptual level. On a practical level, moreover, the empirical component of this project has demonstrated that existing police databases used in the study were incomplete and inappropriate for management and evaluation purposes. The solution to these problems is beyond the scope of this project although recommendations have been made about how they could be improved. In this concluding section some suggestions will be made about indicators which may prove a useful first-step in any pilot study of the performance of police anti-drug strategies and what those indicators should attempt to measure.

There are many issues in performance measurement which should be clarified. Aspects which have already been discussed in section 2 include: the level of analysis (eg. units, forces etc.), periods of analysis (eg. annual or monthly assessment), and the purpose of analysis. At least five questions may be asked within the umbrella of performance measurement, and each requires emphasis on different types of indicators:

- Which police activities produce the best improvements in outcome for society?
- Has the productivity of a particular unit increased over time?
- Which of the units being evaluated has the best productivity?
- To which unit should additional resources be allocated to produce maximum output?
- Should additional resources be devoted to drugs work or other enforcement activity?

The need for indicators at each level of process, output and outcome is worthy of re-iteration. If the outputs and outcomes which could be expected from different types of process were known (such as the effect of a targeted operation against a major dealer of Class A drugs on drugs markets and drug-related crime), then it would be necessary only to monitor changes in process. Alternatively, if the links between output and outcome were known (such as the reduction in the number of drug overdoses which may result from the arrest and conviction of a user-dealer), it would be sufficient to measure only process and outcome. As has been demonstrated in this report, however, these relationships are not known and it is necessary to monitor performance at all three levels. Indeed, the empirical part of this study has demonstrated that even the measurement of process is complex and underdeveloped. The tracking of contextual factors is required due to their influence on the levels of output and outcome which can be expected from different forms of process.

The tracking of output and outcome variables will also be necessary at the aggregate level. The analysis of aggregate series makes attribution to particular elements of police work problematic. One potential way of proceeding would be to predict changes in outcome from measured changes in output, and then investigate whether these expected changes can be traced in the aggregate series. Alternatively, it may be possible to identify 'control' areas or time-periods with which the unit is being evaluated can be compared.

A more robust method of using the indicators would be to trace particular individuals through the system. Currently, this would be time-consuming even within the Criminal Justice System, and greater problems with confidentiality will emerge when the analysis is extended to the health and social care sector. The use of anonymised 'attributors', as demonstrated in section 4, may offer a potential solution.

Many of the factors which have been identified are hard to measure, and information currently available within force is limited. Innovative approaches to information-gathering will be required, such as collaboration with local agencies in contacting panels of experts who have thorough and up-to-date information on changes in drugs markets. In other instances, poor quality or highly subjective information may be available. It will be possible to judge the appropriateness of these estimates and the potential for improvement only when these indicators are pilot-tested in practice. Instruments which are developed in conjunction with those who will use them in practice are likely to be the most feasible and relevant.

This project has demonstrated the complexity of performance measurement in this area, but has also shown that there is potential for the development of meaningful performance indicators. The practical development of these indicators may be a slow and time-consuming process, but in view of the significant amount of resources currently devoted to anti-drugs work, must be justified.

References

Advisory Council on the Misuse of Drugs (1988) *Aids and Drug Misuse Part 1*. London: Department of Health and Social Security.

Agar, M. (1973) *Ripping and Running*. New York: Seminar Press.

Association of Chief Police Officers (ACPO) (1986) *Final Report of the Working Party on Drugs Related Crime* (unpublished).

Ball, J.C. and Ross, A. (1991) *The Effectiveness of Methadone Maintenance Treatment*. New York: Springer-Verlag.

Banks, A. and Waller, T.A.N. (1988) *Drug Misuse: A Practical Handbook for GPs*. Oxford: Blackwell Scientific.

Bean, P. (1991) 'Policing the medical profession: the use of tribunals', in Whynes, D.K. and Bean, P.T. (eds.) *Policing and Prescribing*. London: Macmillan, 60-70.

Bean, P. and Wilkinson, C. (1987) *Drug taking in Nottingham: the links with crime*. Research report to the Home Office Research and Planning Unit.

Bennett, T. and Wright, R. (1986) 'The impact of prescribing on the crimes of opioid users', *British Journal of Addiction*, 81, pp.265-73.

Brecht, M-L., Anglin, M.D. and Wang, J-C (1993) 'Treatment effectiveness for legally coerced versus voluntary methadone maintenance clients', *American Journal of Drug Alcohol Abuse*, 19(1): 89-106.

Burr, A. (1987) 'Chasing the Dragon', *British Journal of Criminology*, 27(4): 333-357.

Chatterton, M.R. (1987) 'Assessing police effectiveness – future propects', *British Journal of Criminology*, Vol 27, No 1, Winter, 1987.

Chatterton, M.R., Frenz S. and Chenery S. (1992) *A Study of Drugs Misuse and its effects in Moss Side, Manchester*. Manchester: Henry Fielding Centre (unpublished Report for Home Office).

Chatterton, M.R. and Frenz, S. (1993) *Evaluation of the Urban Crime Fund Initiative on Merseyside* (unpublished).

Collison, M. (1993) 'Punishing drugs: criminal justice and drug use', *British Journal of Criminology*, 33(3): 382-399.

Department of Health, Scottish Office Home and Health Department and Welsh Office (1991) *Drug Misuse and Dependence: Guidelines on Clinical Management*. London: HMSO

Donoghue, M.C., Stimson, G.V. and Dolan, K.A. (1992) *Syringe Exchange in England: An Overview.* The Centre for Research on Drugs and Health Behaviour: London.

Dorn, N. (1994) 'Three faces of police referral: welfare, justice and business perspectives on multi-agency work with drug arrestees', *Policing and Society*, 4: 13-34.

Dorn, N., Murji, K. and South, N. (1990) 'Drug referral schemes', *Policing*, 6: 482-491.

Dorn, N., Murji, K. and South, N. (1992) *Traffickers: Drug Markets and Law Enforcement.* London: Routledge.

Dupont, R.L. and Greene, M.H. (1972) 'The dynamics of a heroin addiction epidemic', *Science*, 181: 716-722.

Fazey, C. (1988) *Heroin Addiction, Crime and the effects of Medical Treatment.* Report to the Home Office Research and Planning Unit.

Fazey, C. (1991) 'The consequences of illegal drug use', in Whynes, D.K. and Bean, P.T. (eds.) *Policing and Prescribing.* London: Macmillan, 17-34.

Fiddle, S. (1967) *Portraits from a Shooting Gallery.* New York: Harper and Row.

Franey, C., Power, R. and Wells, B. (1993) 'Treatment and services for drug users in Britain', *Journal of Substance Abuse Treatment*, 10: 561-567.

Fraser, A. and George, M. (1988) 'Changing trends in drug use: an initial follow-up of a local heroin using community', *British Journal of Addiction*, 83: 655-663.

Fraser, A. and George, M. (1992) 'Cautions for Cannabis', *Policing*, 8 (2): pp.88-100.

Gilman, M. and Pearson, G. (1991) 'Lifestyles and law enforcement', in Whynes, D.K. and Bean, P.T. (eds.) *Policing and Prescribing.* London: Macmillan, 95-124.

Glanz, A. and Taylor, C. (1987) 'Findings of a national survey of the role of General Practitioners in the treatment of opiate misuse', in Heller, T., Gott, M. and Jeffrey, C. (eds.) *Drug Use and Misuse.* Chichester: John Wiley and Sons.

Glanz, A., Byrne, C., Jackson, P. and Taylor, C. (1989) *The role of community pharmacies in AIDS prevention and drug misuse.* London: Institute of Psychiatry.

Gould, L.C., Walker, A.L., Crane, L.E., and Lidz, C.W. (1974) *Connections: Notes from the Heroin World.* New Haven, USA: Yale University Press.

Griffiths, P., Gossop, M., Powis, B. and Strang, J. (1992) 'Extent and nature of transitions of route among heroin addicts in treatment – preliminary data from the Drug Transitions Study', *British Journal of Addiction*, 87: 485-491.

Hartnoll, R. and Lewis, R. (1984) *The illicit heroin market in Britain: towards a preliminary estimate of national demand.* Mimeo: Drugs Indicator Project. London: University College London.

Hartnoll, R.L., Mitcheson, M.C., Battersby, A., Brown, G., Ellis, M., Fleming, P. and Hedley, N. (1980) 'Evaluation of heroin maintenance in controlled trial', *Archives of General Psychiatry*, 37: 877-884.

Home Office Statistical Department (1985) *Criminal Convictions of Persons first Notified as Narcotic Addicts 1979-81*, Statistical Bulletin 19/85. London: Home Office.

Jarvis, G. and Parker, H. (1988) *Does Medical Treatment Reduce Crime amongst Young Heroin Users?* Report to the Home Office.

Jarvis, G. and Parker, H. (1989) 'Young heroin users and crime', *British Journal of Criminology*, 29(2): 175-185.

Kay, L. (no date given) *Problem Drug Users in Custody – Information, Advice and Treatment.* Manchester: Lifeline Project Ltd.

Lart, R. and Stimson, G.V. (1990) 'National survey of syringe exchange schemes in England', *British Journal of Addiction*, 85: 1433-1443.

Levine, D., Stoloff, P. and Spruill, N. (1976) 'Public drug treatment and addict crime', *Journal of Legal Studies*, 5(2): 435-462.

Lewis, R., Hartnoll, R., Bryer, S., Daviaud, E. and Mitcheson, M. (1985) 'Scoring smack: the illicit heroin market in London 1980-1983', *British Journal of Addiction*, 80: 281-290.

Lord President of the Council, et al (1994) *Tackling Drugs Together: A consultation document on a strategy for England 1995-1998.* Cm 2678. London: HMSO.

Moore, M.H. (1977) *Buy and Bust.* Lexington, USA: D.C. Heath and Company.

Mott, J. (1981) 'Criminal involvements and penal response', in Edwards, G.E. and Busch, C. (eds.) *Drug Problems in Britain.* London: Academic Press.

Mott, J. (1986) 'Opiate use and burglary', *British Journal of Addiction*. 81: 671-677.

Mott, J. (1991) 'Crime and Heroin Use', in Whynes, D.K. and Bean, P.T. (eds.) *Policing and Prescribing*. London: Macmillan, 77-94.

Niskanen, W.A. (1992) 'Economists and drug policy'. *Carnegie-Rochester Conference Series on Public Policy*, 36: 223-248.

Parker, H. and Newcombe, R. (1987) 'Heroin Use and Acquisitive Crime in an English Community', *British Journal of Sociology*, 38: pp.331-50.

Parker, H., Bakx, K. and Newcombe, N. (1988) *Living with Heroin*. Milton Keynes: Open University Press.

Pearson, G. (1990) 'Drugs, law enforcement and criminology', in Berridge, V. (ed.) *Drugs Research and Policy in Britain*. Avebury: Aldershot.

Ramsay, M. (1994) 'Troubling Riddles', *Drugs Prevention News*.

Roumasset, J. and Hadreas, J. (1977) 'Addicts, fences, and the market for stolen goods', *Public Finance Quarterly*, 5(2): 247-272.

Senay, E.C. (1985) 'Methadone maintenance treatment', *International Journal of the Addictions*, 20(6&7): 803-821.

Silverman, L., Spruill, N. and Levine, D. (1975) *Urban Crime and Availability*. Centre for Naval Analysis: Public Research Institute Report 75-1, Washington, DC.

Southwark Arrest Referral Pilot Project Monitoring Group (no date given) *Report to the Home Office on the Southwark Arrest Referral Pilot Project, January 1989 to 1991*. London: Southwark Arrest Referral Pilot Project Monitoring Group (unpublished report).

Strang, J. (1989) 'A model service: turning the generalist on to drugs', in McGregor, S. (ed.) *Drugs and British Society*. London: Routledge.

Tantam, D., Donmall, M., Webster, A. and Strang, J. (1993) 'Do general practitioners and general psychiatrists want to look after drug misusers? Evaluation of a non-specialist treatment policy', *British Journal of General Practice*, 43: 470-474.

Thorley, A. (1987) 'Longitudinal studies of drug dependence', in Edwards, G. and Busch, C. (eds.) *Drug Problems in Britain: A Review of Ten Years*. London: Academic Press.

Walters, G. (1994) *Drugs and Crime in lifestyle perspective*.

Watson, P. (1985) *The Fate of Drug Addicts on a Waiting List*. Report to the North Western Regional Health Authority.

Wright, A and Waymont, A. (1989) *Drug Enforcement Strategies and Intelligence Needs*, mimeo. London: ACPO/Police Foundation.

White, M.D. and Luksetich, W.A. (1983) 'Heroin: price elasticity and enforcement strategies', *Economic Inquiry*, 21: 557-564.

Whynes, D. (1991) 'Drug problems, drug policies', in Whynes, D.K. and Bean, P.T. (eds.) *Policing and Prescribing*. London: Macmillan, 1-14.

Wright, A. Waymont, A. and Gregory, F.E. (1993) *Drugs Squads: Drugs Law Enforcement and Intelligence in England and Wales*. London: Police Foundation.

RECENT PAPERS IN THE CRIME DETECTION AND PREVENTION SERIES

55. **Witness Intimidation: Strategies for prevention.** Warwick Maynard. 1994.

56. **Preventing Vandalism: What Works?** Mary Barker and Cressida Bridgeman. 1994.

57. **Thinking About Crime Prevention Performance Indicators.** Nick Tilley. 1995.

58. **Combating Burglary: An Evaluation of Three Strategies.** Janet Stockdale and Peter Gresham. 1995.

59. **Biting Back: Tackling Repeat Burglary and Car Crime.** David Anderson, Sylvia Chenery and Ken Pease. 1995.

60. **Policing and Neighbourhood Watch: Strategic Issues.** Gloria Laycock and Nick Tilley. 1995.

61. **Investigating, seizing and confiscating the proceeds of crime.** Michael Levi and Lisa Osofsky. 1995.